To Angela,
Best Wishes.
Debbie 2011.

Debbie Brown's

BABY cakes

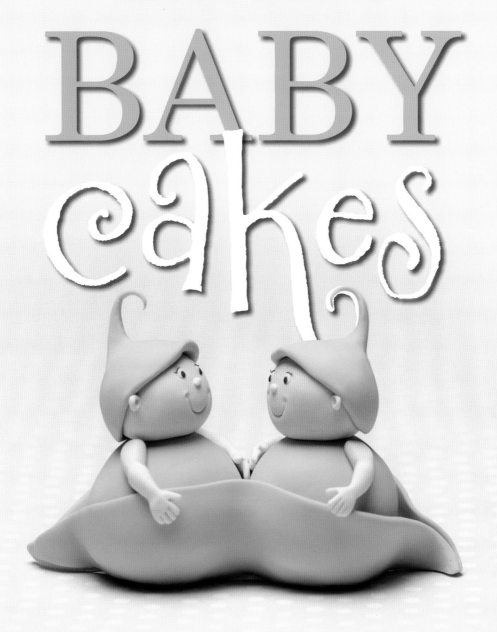

adorable cakes for christenings,
birthdays and baby showers

Dedication

For Hannah

I wrote this book for you, but you probably won't be interested in that until you're all grown and you look back at the pictures of your special birthday cakes over the years showing Nanna in the background looking on proudly. But perhaps one day, when you're a beautiful young girl, you'll pull it off the bookshelf, give it a little dust and take a proper look inside, for every one designed herein I was thinking of you. x

First published in September 2011 by
B. Dutton Publishing Limited, The Grange,
Hones Yard, Farnham, Surrey, GU9 8BB.
Copyright: Debra Brown 2011
ISBN-13: 978-1-905113-28-6
All rights reserved.

Publisher: Beverley Dutton
Editor: Jenny Stewart
Art Director/Designer: Sarah Ryan
Deputy Editor: Jenny Royle
Designer: Zena Manicom
Sub Editor/Graphic Designer: Louise Pepé
PR and Advertising Manager: Natalie Bull
Photography: Alister Thorpe
Printed in China

Wallpapers supplied by wallpaperdirect.co.uk

Disclaimer
The Author and Publisher have made every effort to ensure that the contents of this book, if followed carefully, will not cause harm or injury or pose any danger. Please note that some inedible items, such as lolly sticks and cake dowels, have been used in the recipes in this book. All such inedible items must be removed before the cakes are eaten. Similarly, any non food-grade equipment and substances must not come into contact with any food that is to be eaten. Neither the Author nor the Publisher can be held responsible for errors or omissions and cannot accept liability for injury, damage or loss to persons or property, however it may arise, as a result of acting upon guidelines and information printed in this book.

introduction

I have written many titles over the years but my favourites by far are books that include cakes for children and sculpture, so this was especially nice to write. What a wonderful subject matter to base a cake book on, the arrival of a newborn, babies, small children and all their special celebrations.

With a plethora of subject matter, I had such fun dreaming up these sculptures and cake designs. Although I had lots of ideas with bright colours, when it came down to it I chose pretty, soft pastel shades, mostly in the typical baby colours of pink, blue and lemon. Any of these designs could be made with brighter, more fun colour tones and I've made sure throughout the book there are alternatives to show the different look you can get just by changing one thing.

I've always been very careful, especially with the earlier books, not to make things look too difficult. I'm sure even with the simple and easy books I've written there are many readers who have picked the book up in the store and then popped it back on the shelf thinking they couldn't possibly make any of the cakes! But please don't panic thinking it's impossible to produce something to be proud of because I promise it is not.

Although I could have filled the book twice over there had to be a cut-off point, so I made sure every one that was included would be achievable for every level of expertise, even total beginners. I have often found throughout my years of teaching that it really doesn't matter if you have no experience at all – although of course it helps, I find natural ability always shines through. With the clear step-by-step instructions and photographs to help, you'll finish with a cake to be proud of.

Debbie

Acknowledgements

I always have to thank firstly my family, for suffering the long days and nights whilst I'm working, for their patience and understanding and most of all their unending support and encouragement.

Thank you to Alister Thorpe for the beautiful pictures throughout this book. Although the camera never lies it takes a certain skill to capture to the best advantage.

Whenever I write a book with B. Dutton Publishing I always look forward to working with Jenny Stewart and Sarah Ryan. I can't sing their praises highly enough and thank them profusely for their talent, enthusiasm and in this case also their understanding and patience.

contents

recipes and baking charts

Butter Sponge Cake

Nothing tastes quite like a butter sponge cake and it is versatile enough to complement many different flavours and fillings. This recipe has a little extra flour to make it slightly firmer for sculpting and the addition of buttermilk makes the sponge moist with a rich and smooth taste.

Basic variations for butter sponge cake

Chocolate marble cake

Before spooning the cake mixture into the bakeware, fold in 200g (7oz) of melted chocolate until marbled. For a light chocolate cake, fold in the chocolate completely.

Chocolate orange marble cake

Make as per the chocolate marble cake and add the grated rind and juice of one organic orange.

Lemon cake

Add the grated rind and juice of one organic lemon to the cake mixture.

Orange and lemon cake

Add the grated rind of an organic orange and lemon to the cake mixture and a squeeze of orange juice.

Coffee cake

Add 2 tablespoons of coffee essence to the cake mixture.

Almond cake

Add 1 teaspoon of almond essence and 2-3 tablespoons of ground almonds to the cake mixture.

1 Preheat the oven to 150°C/300°F/gas mark 2, then grease and line the bakeware.

2 Sift the self-raising flour into a bowl.

3 Soften the butter and place in a food mixer or large mixing bowl with the caster/superfine sugar. Beat until the mixture is pale and fluffy.

4 Add the eggs to the mixture one at a time with a spoonful of the flour, beating well after each addition.

5 Using a spatula or large spoon, fold the remaining flour into the mixture.

6 Gently stir in the vanilla extract and buttermilk.

7 Spoon the mixture into the bakeware then make a dip in the top of the mixture using the back of a spoon. If you are using more than one tin, make sure each one is evenly filled; if you are making cupcakes, ½ to ¾ fill each cupcake case.

8 Bake in the centre of the oven for the recommended time or until a skewer inserted in the centre comes out clean.

9 Leave to cool in the bakeware for five minutes, then turn out onto a wire rack and leave to cool completely. When cold, store in an airtight container or double wrap in cling film (plastic wrap) for at least eight hours, allowing the texture to settle before use.

Cake project	Bakeware	Unsalted butter, softened	Caster (superfine) sugar, sifted	Large eggs	Self-raising flour, sifted	Vanilla extract	Buttermilk	Baking time
20 Cupcakes	Cupcake cases	225g (8oz)	225g (8oz)	4	225g (8oz)	5ml (1tsp)	15ml (1tbsp)	20 minutes
Wash Day	2 x 15cm (6") and 1 x 10cm (4") round tins	400g (14oz)	400g (14oz)	7	510g (1lb 2oz)	5ml (1tsp)	75ml (4tbsp)	1-1¼ hours
Stork Delivery	1 x 20cm (8"), 1 x 15cm (6") and 1 x 10cm (4") round tins	455g (1lb)	455g (1lb)	8	565g (1lb 4oz)	5ml (1tsp)	75ml (4tbsp)	50 minutes - 1¼ hours
Mother's Love	1 x 20cm (8") round cake tin	285g (10oz)	285g (10oz)	5	340g (12oz)	5ml (1tsp)	55ml (3tbsp)	1¼-1½ hours
Crying Babies	1 x 20cm (8") and 1 x 10cm (4") round tins	340g (12oz)	340g (12oz)	6	430g (15oz)	5ml (1tsp)	55ml (3tbsp)	50 minutes - 1¼ hours
Pea in a Pod	2 x 15cm (6") bowl-shaped tins/ovenproof bowls	340g (12oz)	340g (12oz)	6	430g (15oz)	5ml (1tsp)	55ml (3tbsp)	1-1¼ hours
Toy Box	2 x 15cm (6") square tins	340g (12oz)	340g (12oz)	6	430g (15oz)	5ml (1tsp)	55ml (3tbsp)	1-1¼ hours
Bears	2 x 15cm (6"), 2 x 10cm (4") and 2 x 7cm (2¾") bowl-shaped tins/ovenproof bowls	455g (1lb)	455g (1lb)	8	565g (1lb 4oz)	5ml (1tsp)	75ml (4tbsp)	1-1¼ hours
Blue Fairytale Castle	1 x 15cm (6") square and 1 x 10cm (4") round tins	340g (12oz)	340g (12oz)	6	430g (15oz)	5ml (1tsp)	55ml (3tbsp)	1-1¼ hours
Pink Fairytale Castle	1 x 18cm (7") and 1 x 10cm (4") round tins	340g (12oz)	340g (12oz)	6	430g (15oz)	5ml (1tsp)	55ml (3tbsp)	1-1¼ hours
Baby Blocks	1 x 20cm (8") and 2 x 10cm (4") square tins	340g (12oz)	340g (12oz)	6	430g (15oz)	5ml (1tsp)	55ml (3tbsp)	1-1¼ hours
Cute Kittens	1 x 30cm (10") square tin	400g (14oz)	400g (14oz)	7	510g (1lb 2oz)	5ml (1tsp)	75ml (4tbsp)	1¼-1½ hours
Baby's First Doll	20cm (8") round tin and 15cm (6") dome-shaped tin/ovenproof bowl	400g (14oz)	400g (14oz)	7	510g (1lb 2oz)	5ml (1tsp)	75ml (4tbsp)	1¼-1½ hours
Noah's Ark	1 x 20cm (8") round tin, 1 x 20cm (8") bowl-shaped tin/ovenproof bowl and 2 x 10cm (4") square tins	565g (1lb 4oz)	565g (1lb 4oz)	10	650g (1lb 7oz)	10ml (2tsp)	90ml (5tbsp)	1¼-1½ hours

Devil's Chocolate Cake

This recipe won't disappoint as it bakes well with an even and easy-to-sculpt texture that keeps exceptionally rich and moist.

1 Preheat the oven to 160°C/325°F/gas mark 3.

2 Make the coffee in a heat-resistant bowl. Break the dark chocolate into small pieces, add to the coffee and stir until melted. Leave to cool.

3 Beat the softened butter and dark brown sugar together until light and fluffy. Gradually add the eggs one at a time, then stir in the vanilla extract and the cooled chocolate/coffee mixture.

4 Sift the plain flour and bicarbonate of soda together and gradually fold into the mixture a little at a time until well blended and the mixture is smooth. Stir in the soured cream.

5 Spoon the mixture into the bakeware then make a dip in the top of the mixture using the back of a spoon. If you are using more than one tin, make sure each one is evenly filled; if you are making cupcakes, ½ to ¾ fill each cupcake case.

6 Bake in the centre of the oven for the recommended time or until a skewer inserted in the centre comes out clean.

7 Leave to cool in the bakeware for five minutes, then turn out onto a wire rack and leave to cool completely. When cold, store in an airtight container or double wrap in cling film (plastic wrap) for at least eight hours, allowing the texture to settle before use.

Cake project	Bakeware	Hot, strong black coffee	Dark couverture chocolate	Unsalted butter, softened	Soft, dark brown sugar	Large eggs	Plain flour (sifted)	Bicar- bonate of soda	Vanilla extract	Soured cream	Baking time
30 Cupcakes	Cupcake cases	175ml (6fl oz)	75g (2½oz)	175g (6oz)	280g (9¾oz)	3	280g (9¾oz)	7ml (1½tsp)	5ml (1tsp)	175ml (6fl oz)	20 minutes
Wash Day	2 x 15cm (6") and 1 x 10cm (4") round tins	290ml (10¼fl oz)	125g (4½oz)	290g (10¼oz)	470g (1lb ½oz)	5	470g (1lb ½oz)	10ml (2tsp)	10ml (2tsp)	290ml (10¼fl oz)	1-1¼ hours
Stork Delivery	1 x 20cm (8"), 1 x 15cm (6") and 1 x 10cm (4") round tins	350ml (12¼fl oz)	150g (5¼oz)	350g (12¼oz)	550g (1lb 3½oz)	6	550g (1lb 3½oz)	15ml (3tsp)	10ml (2tsp)	350ml (12¼fl oz)	1¼ -1½ hours
Mother's Love ✈	1 x 20cm (8") round cake tin	175ml (6fl oz)	75g (2½oz)	175g (6oz)	280g (9¾oz)	3	280g (9¾oz)	7ml (1½tsp)	5ml (1tsp)	175ml (6fl oz)	1¼ -1½ hours
Crying Babies	1 x 20cm (8") and 1 x 10cm (4") round tins	235ml (8¼fl oz)	100g (3½oz)	235g (8¼oz)	375g (13¼oz)	4	375g (13¼oz)	10ml (2tsp)	10ml (2tsp)	235ml (8¼fl oz)	1-1¼ hours
Pea in a Pod	2 x 15cm (6") bowl-shaped tins/ovenproof bowls	235ml (8¼fl oz)	100g (3½oz)	235g (8¼oz)	375g (13¼oz)	4	375g (13¼oz)	10ml (2tsp)	10ml (2tsp)	235ml (8¼fl oz)	1¼ -1½ hours
Toy Box	2 x 15cm (6") square tins	175ml (6fl oz)	75g (2½oz)	175g (6oz)	280g (9¾oz)	3	280g (9¾oz)	7ml (1½tsp)	5ml (1tsp)	175ml (6fl oz)	1-1¼ hours
Bears	2 x 15cm (6"), 2 x 10cm (4") and 2 x 7cm (2¾") bowl-shaped tins/ ovenproof bowls	350ml (12¼fl oz)	150g (5¼oz)	350g (12¼oz)	550g (1lb 3½oz)	6	550g (1lb 3½oz)	15ml (3tsp)	10ml (2tsp)	350ml (12¼fl oz)	1-1½ hours
Blue Fairytale Castle	1 x 15cm (6") square and 1 x 10cm (4") round tins	175ml (6fl oz)	75g (2½oz)	175g (6oz)	280g (9¾oz)	3	280g (9¾oz)	7ml (1½tsp)	5ml (1tsp)	175ml (6fl oz)	1-1¼ hours
Pink Fairytale Castle	1 x 18cm (7") and 1 x 10cm (4") round tins	175ml (6fl oz)	75g (2½oz)	175g (6oz)	280g (9¾oz)	3	280g (9¾oz)	7ml (1½tsp)	5ml (1tsp)	175ml (6fl oz)	1-1¼ hours
Baby Blocks	1 x 20cm (8") and 2 x 10cm (4") square tins	235ml (8¼fl oz)	100g (3½oz)	235g (8¼oz)	375g (13¼oz)	4	375g (13¼oz)	10ml (2tsp)	10ml (2tsp)	235ml (8¼fl oz)	1-1¼ hours
Cute Kittens	1 x 30cm (10") square tin	290ml (10¼fl oz)	125g (4½oz)	290g (10¼oz)	470g (1lb ½oz)	5	470g (1lb ½oz)	10ml (2tsp)	10ml (2tsp)	290ml (10¼fl oz)	1¼ -1½ hours
Baby's First Doll	20cm (8") round tin and 15cm (6") dome-shaped tin/ovenproof bowl	290ml (10¼fl oz)	125g (4½oz)	290g (10¼oz)	470g (1lb ½oz)	5	470g (1lb ½oz)	10ml (2tsp)	10ml (2tsp)	290ml (10¼fl oz)	1¼ -1½ hours
Noah's Ark	1 x 20cm (8") round tin, 1 x 20cm (8") bowl-shaped tin/ovenproof bowl and 2 x 10cm (4") square tins	350ml (12¼fl oz)	150g (5¼oz)	350g (12¼oz)	550g (1lb 3½oz)	6	550g (1lb 3½oz)	15ml (3tsp)	10ml (2tsp)	350ml (12¼fl oz)	1-1½ hours

Marshmallow Rice Cereal

This is not only a quick and easy, bake-free recipe that makes delicious treats, but it is also used by cake decorators as a substitute for cake in small areas of a particular design that need to be lightweight but still strong. Cake with filling can be heavy and may cause pressure and possible damage to the cake below it.

This recipe can also be used for some of the mini projects throughout the book, especially the ball shaped designs, as it's easy to roll and when left to set is a sturdy but tasty treat that is easy to decorate.

Ingredients

50g (1¾oz) unsalted butter
200g (7oz) white marshmallows
160g (5½oz) crisped rice cereal

Makes approximately 350g-380g
(12¼oz-13½oz)

1 Melt the butter in large saucepan over a low heat. Add the marshmallows and stir constantly until melted. Stir for a further minute. Remove from the heat, add the cereal and stir until well coated.

2 Allow to cool slightly and then mould into the required shape, compacting it by pressing firmly to create a smooth surface. You will need to work quickly before it sets hard.

Cake Truffles

Cake truffle is a mixture of cake crumbs, usually leftover trimmings from the main cake, mixed together with any cake filling, enough to make the crumbs moist and easily rolled into the required shape. You can also add ingredients like chocolate chips, mixed nuts and, for an extra touch, flavour with a liqueur. My favourite is chocolate cake crumbs with a little chocolate ganache and a dash of orange liqueur, closely followed by butter sponge crumbs mixed with vanilla buttercream and a little zest and juice from an organic lemon.

Cake truffle is great to use on areas of cake that would be difficult to sculpt or bake, usually because of the size required. They have the same weight as cake and filling though, so aren't suitable for areas of cake that need something lighter in weight so as not to damage the main cake (such as Baby Pea's head, page 53). However, they are perfect if you'd like to substitute a modelled item of sugarpaste like the heads on the mini doll cakes (see page 100). These take 60g of sugarpaste for each head if they are made entirely from paste but if cake truffle is used and then covered with sugarpaste, the amount of covering is greatly reduced and they are much more delicious!

You can also use this recipe to make cake pops – simply roll into a ball, insert a lolly stick then dip into melted chocolate or your choice of coating.

The basic recipe below is extremely simple to make.

Ingredients

150g (5¼oz) cake crumbs
50g (1¾oz) cake filling

Makes approximately 200g (7oz)

1 Place the cake into a food processor with a dough hook and mix on a slow speed until crumbly. Add your choice of cake filling and flavour and then mix slowly until combined and mixed to a stiff ball. If the mixture is still crumbly add a little more cake filling until combined.

2 Break off the amount required and mould into the required shape. Refrigerate until firm. Before covering with sugarpaste you will need to brush the surface with a little cooled, boiled water or sugar syrup so the sugarpaste sticks.

Sugar Syrup (Moistening Syrup)

For butter sponge cake and variations

Sugar syrup is an easy way to ensure your cake remains moist during the preparation process and, of course, the serving. When preparing your cake, brush or dab sugar syrup carefully over each sponge cake layer, preferably with a silicone pastry brush and before the cake filling is added. The syrup slowly soaks into the sponge until it is distributed evenly throughout the cake. I also brush syrup over the top and sides of the sponge cake just before the crumb coat is spread over the surface as I find it spreads a little easier.

Some cake decorators prefer to be generous when brushing on the syrup whilst others are more conservative – it purely depends on personal choice. I find excessive sugar syrup can cause the sponge to become very sweet, so I recommend the following quantity for a 25cm (10") cake. You can, of course, add more; in fact, many cake decorators use double this quantity.

Ingredients

115g (4oz) caster (superfine) sugar
125ml (4½fl oz) water
5ml (1tsp) flavouring (optional)

Makes 240ml (8½fl oz)

1 Pour the measured sugar into a saucepan along with the water. Heat gently and bring to the boil, stirring carefully. Do not leave unattended as sugar can burn easily. Simmer for one minute to ensure all the sugar granules have dissolved completely. Remove from the heat and set aside to cool.

2 Store in an airtight container and refrigerate. Use within one month.

3 Flavouring sugar syrup is not absolutely necessary but if you've baked a flavoured sponge cake then flavouring the sugar syrup to complement it can really enhance the taste. Although the most popular flavouring is vanilla, different seedless fruit jams also work very well.

Buttercream

A great versatile filling and the first choice for many, buttercream made with real unsalted butter is delicious as I find the flavour much creamier than when using salted butter. I add milk as this makes the buttercream paler in colour and much lighter in texture, but if you prefer a firmer, yellow buttercream you can omit the milk and add a little less icing sugar. The basic recipe can be flavoured if required to suit your preference.

Ingredients

175g (6oz) unsalted butter, softened
30ml-45ml (2tbsp-3tbsp) milk
5ml (1tsp) flavouring (optional)
450g (1lb) icing sugar, sifted

Makes approximately 625g (1lb 6oz)

1 Place the softened butter, milk and flavouring into a mixer. Mix on medium speed and add the icing sugar a little at

a time. Mix until light, fluffy and pale in colour.

2 Store in an airtight container and use within 10 days. Bring to room temperature and beat again before use.

Basic variations for buttercream

Chocolate
Fold in 145g-200g (5oz-7oz) of melted and cooled dark, milk or white chocolate.

Orange or lemon
Add 30ml-45ml (2-3 level tbsp) of orange or lemon curd.

Coffee
Add 30ml-45ml (2tbsp-3tbsp) of coffee essence.

Raspberry
Add 30ml-45ml (2-3 level tbsp) of seedless raspberry jam.

Almond
Add 5ml (1tsp) of almond essence.

Chocolate Ganache

Ganache is a rich chocolate filling and coating that sets firm, giving a good surface for the sugarpaste covering. Leave for 24 hours to set at room temperature or refrigerate overnight. When you're ready to use the ganache, bring back to room temperature and beat well.

The recipes below make enough for the projects in the book, plus a little extra just in case.

Ingredients

300g (10½oz) dark couverture chocolate
300ml (10½fl oz) fresh whipping or double cream

Makes around 520g-540g (1lb 2oz)

400g (14oz) dark couverture chocolate
400ml (14fl oz) fresh whipping or double cream

Makes around 720g-740g (1lb 10oz)

1 Melt the chocolate in a bowl over a pan of hot water (or a bain-marie) to 40°C (105°F).

2 Pour the cream into a saucepan and bring to a simmer for two to three minutes. Allow the cream to cool slightly for around five minutes and then whisk the cream into the melted chocolate until well combined. The mixture should be thick and glossy.

3 Allow the ganache to cool completely and then transfer into an airtight container and refrigerate. Use within one month.

Sugarpaste (Rolled Fondant)

Sugarpaste (also known as rolled fondant) is readily available throughout the UK in supermarkets and cake decorating outlets. Each brand has a slightly different texture, taste and working quality, so try different brands to find which suits you best. If you prefer to make your own, I would recommend the recipe below.

Ingredients

1 egg white made up from dried egg albumen
30ml (2tbsp) liquid glucose
625g (1lb 6oz) icing (confectioner's) sugar
A little white vegetable fat (shortening), if required
A pinch of CMC powder*

Makes 625g (1lb 6oz)

* NOTE: CMC is an abbreviation of Carboxy Methyl Cellulose, an edible thickener widely used in the food industry. The CMC you use must be food grade. Brand names include SK CMC, Debbie Brown's Magic Powder (CMC), Tylose, Tylopur, Tylo and Sugarcel. Alternatively, you can use SK Gum Tragacanth, which is a natural product.

1 Put the egg white and liquid glucose into a bowl, using a warm spoon for the liquid glucose.

2 Sift the icing sugar into the bowl, adding a little at a time and stirring until the mixture thickens.

3 Turn the mixture out onto a work surface dusted liberally with icing sugar and knead the paste until soft, smooth and pliable. If the paste is slightly dry and cracked, fold in a little white vegetable fat and knead again. If the paste is very soft and sticky, add a little more icing sugar. Add a pinch of CMC to strengthen the paste.

4 Transfer the paste immediately into a food-grade polythene bag and store in an airtight container. Keep the paste cool, either at room temperature, or in the refrigerator if the atmosphere is warm. Bring back to room temperature and knead thoroughly before use.

To save time when decorating a cake, homemade sugarpaste can be frozen for up to three months. Allow to defrost thoroughly at room temperature before use.

Royal Icing

Royal icing is used to pipe fine details and to stick sugar pieces together: when dry it will hold items firmly in place. Ready-made royal icing can be obtained from supermarkets or in powder form (follow the instructions on the packet). If you prefer to make your own, you can follow this recipe.

Ingredients

5ml (1 level tsp) egg albumen
15ml (3tsp) cooled, boiled water
65g-70g (2¼oz) icing (confectioner's) sugar

Makes 75g (2½oz)

1 Put the egg albumen into a bowl. Add the water and stir until dissolved.

2 Beat in the icing sugar a little at a time until the icing is firm, glossy and forms peaks if a spoon is pulled out.

3 To stop the icing forming a crust, place a damp cloth over the top of the bowl until you are ready to use it or transfer to an airtight container and refrigerate.

Modelling Paste

This quick and easy recipe makes a high quality modelling paste. If you are short of time or prefer to use a ready-made paste, SK Mexican Modelling Paste is ready-to-use and gives good results.

Ingredients

450g (1lb) sugarpaste
5ml (1 level tsp) CMC powder

Makes 450g (1lb)

Knead the CMC into the sugarpaste. The sugarpaste will start to thicken as soon as the CMC is incorporated so can be used immediately. The paste will continue to thicken gradually over a period of 24 hours. The amount of CMC can be varied depending on usage and on the room temperature and humidity, so adjust accordingly to achieve the required consistency. Store in an airtight container.

Edible Glue

This recipe makes a strong sugar glue which works extremely well. Alternatively, ready-made sugar glue can be purchased from specialist cake decorating outlets.

Ingredients

1.25ml (¼tsp) CMC powder
30ml (2tbsp) boiled water, cooled until warm

Makes 30ml (2tbsp)

1 Mix the CMC powder with the warm water and leave to stand until the powder has fully dissolved. The glue should be smooth and have a soft dropping consistency. If the glue thickens after a few days, add a few more drops of pre-boiled water.

2 Store in an airtight container in the refrigerator and use within one week.

3 To use, brush a thin coat over the surface of the item you wish to glue, leave for a few moments to become tacky, then press the item in place.

Pastillage Sugar Sticks

These are cut or rolled lengths of pastillage, a fast-drying paste that keeps its shape and dries extremely hard. Sugar sticks are used as edible supports, mainly to help hold modelled heads in place. If you are short of time, you can use strands of dried, raw spaghetti for smaller pieces or paper lolly sticks where more support is required. Whichever option you choose, remember to remove the supports before the figures are eaten.

Ingredients

5ml (1 level tsp) royal icing, made to stiff-peak consistency
1.25ml (¼tsp) CMC
Icing sugar in sugar shaker

Makes approximately 10-20 sugar sticks

1 Mix the CMC into the royal icing until the mixture thickens and forms a paste. If the paste is slightly wet, knead in a little icing sugar until the paste is soft and pliable.

2 Either roll out the paste and cut into different sized strips of various lengths using a plain-bladed knife, or roll individual sausages of paste to the sizes required. Leave to dry, preferably overnight on a sheet of food-grade foam sponge. When completely dry, store in an airtight container.

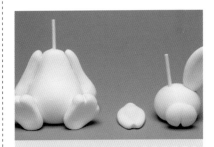

tip

These can be used instead of paper lolly sticks wherever they are listed in the book. Do bear in mind, however, that the lolly sticks are slightly stronger so will support more weight and, unlike sugar, they do not absorb moisture when working in humidity.

basic equipment

There is a wide variety of equipment available to help you achieve brilliant results with your cake designs. If you already have sugarcraft tools or you have a good local supplier, please feel free to make the most of the items you have. I am well known for not using much equipment, and I always bear in mind that there may be readers from other countries who may not have the choice that we have here in the UK. I usually only use what is absolutely necessary and specialist equipment that I would highly recommend – items that I use over and over again which are favourites in my small workbox.

Each project gives a list of what you will require to decorate the cake, but the items here will give you the basics to get started. A list of recommended suppliers is given on page 112.

1 Bakeware/cupcake cases

Cake tins are available to buy or hire from sugarcraft shops in a huge range of shapes and sizes. For smaller cakes, choose from oven-safe bowls, flexible silicone bakeware, mini cake pans and cupcake cases, depending on the project you are making.

2 Ball tool or bone tool

When pushed into soft paste a ball tool indents a smooth, neat circle. A bone tool can do this also but if the back of the tool is used it can also indent a teardrop. Both tools are useful for figure and animal modelling.

3 Cake drums, boards and cards

15mm thick cake drums, often referred to as cake boards, are food safe and lightweight but strong enough to hold the weight of a heavy cake. The thinner boards (5mm) are still strong and can be used as an alternative to cake drums if preferred. Cake cards, which are thinner still, are used between stacked cakes (to support the dowelling) and underneath mini cakes to protect the surface underneath. Depending on which are available, I recommend you cover these with a double layer of cling film (plastic wrap) to prevent them going soft with moisture from your cake. Another alternative is to use pizza boards as these have a food-grade covering on both sides. In the US, you may find that food-grade foam boards or plastic plates are more readily available. As long as the separator is safe to use with food it does not matter which you choose.

4 Cake smoothers

These will help to create a smooth, professional finish when covering cakes and boards with sugarpaste. It is useful to have two so that you can hold one in each hand, especially if you want to create neat edges as you can press on opposite sides.

5 Cutters

There are many different cutters available – I tend to use basic flower shapes (blossoms, rose petals and daisies) and simple shapes (such as circles, hearts and squares). Plunger cutters are ideal for tiny shapes. Where specific cutters are required you will find these listed with each project.

6 Dowelling rods

These are invaluable as supports for large cakes and can also be used as internal supports for large modelled items. I always use plastic rather than wooden dowels. The number of dowels you need is listed with each project, but it is always useful to have a few in your workbox.

7 Fine, pointed scissors

These can be used to snip small pieces of hair on your modelled figures, or use to cut fingers and toes instead of a knife.

8 Non-stick board

Although not a necessity it is easier to roll out sugarpaste on a non-stick surface. A non-stick board will still need a sprinkling of icing sugar to prevent sticking but I find

you use much less than if you are working on a kitchen surface.

9 Paintbrushes

I always use good quality artists' paintbrushes as these hold paint and sugar glue well and the hairs do not mark the surface of sugarpaste. I also use brushes to pick up small items so as not to squash them. A range of sizes is available from your local sugarcraft shop – use the round brushes for painting and the flat brushes for dusting (specific requirements are given with each project).

10 Paint palette

A paint palette is always useful for colour mixing as well as for holding small amounts of glue, water or clear spirit.

11 Palette knives (straight and cranked)

A straight palette knife is useful for spreading the cake filling/crumb coat over a cake. If you use a cranked palette knife for this, ensure you use the back (hold the curve of the blade upwards). A cranked palette knife is also useful for lifting small pieces from the non-stick board/work surface.

12 Paper lolly sticks

These are very useful for supporting heads on figures; they are smaller than dowels but stronger than sugar sticks or spaghetti (see page 15). Always remember to safely remove any inedible supports before the cake is eaten.

13 Piping bags

Parchment piping bags are needed when you are using royal icing and for injecting filling into a small cake or cupcake. You can buy them ready-made from sugarcraft shops or make your own if you prefer. They can be used on their own or with a nozzle (see below).

14 Piping nozzles (various sizes)

Various sizes of plain piping nozzles are used throughout the book, either for piping or to cut out tiny circles. The sizes required are specified in the equipment list with each project.

15 Pointed modelling tool or CelStick

Although most paintbrush handles have a tapered end which I often use to indent paste (ideal as most sugarcrafters will have one in their workbox), a pointed modelling tool or CelStick is useful to have: it is similar in shape but the material in which it is made is smooth and non-stick.

16 Ribbon

To make your cakes look professional, always edge the cake board at the base with co-ordinating ribbon. 15mm-width ribbon fits a cake drum perfectly and can be attached with a non-toxic glue stick or double-sided tape (see page 21).

17 Rolling pins

Large and small polypropylene rolling pins are a good investment as they are durable and will last for years if looked after well. Use a large one for rolling out cake coverings and a small one for smaller decorations.

18 Ruler

It is always useful to have a ruler to hand so you can be accurate when carving and decorating cakes. Keep one for sugarcraft use only.

19 Small, plain-bladed knife and large, serrated knife

You will need a small knife to cut and trim ready-to-roll pastes (such as sugarpaste and modelling paste). Make sure the handle doesn't impede your movement when cutting. A large, serrated knife is needed for cutting a cake before filling.

20 Sugar shaker

This isn't an absolute necessity as icing (confectioner's) sugar could easily be sprinkled by hand, but as it is very useful when rolling out paste. Choose a shaker with generous holes in the lid.

21 Turntable

A turntable allows you work on the sides of a cake without having to handle it. Make sure the turntable you choose has a good height, i.e. elevates your work to a level that you are comfortable with. Metal turntables are the most sturdy but well-made plastic ones are the most readily available. All turntables can hold a good weight but make sure the one you use keeps the cake level without rocking from side to side.

There are a few other items of equipment that you may find useful:

- Cake leveller/layer cutter, to make sure the cakes are level before filling.

- Cocktail sticks, for frilling pastes and making tiny holes. They are also useful for colouring pastes (see page 23).

- Craft knife, for cutting small pieces of modelling paste.

- Food-grade foam sponge, for drying pieces of sugar on.

- Pastry brush, for spreading sugar syrup and cake filling.

basic techniques

All of the projects in this book require the cake to be layered, filled and crumb-coated with your chosen filling (see pages 12 to 13). Following these basic instructions will give you a level surface on which to work, allowing you to achieve the best possible results when the cake is decorated. I have also given guidelines for a few other basic cake decorating techniques to help you achieve great results.

Preparing a Sponge Cake

1 Trim the crust from the cake and level the top with a serrated knife or cake leveller. Cut two to four layers in the cake (a quick and easy way is to use a cake leveller, which can also be used to cut as many layers as you wish extremely easily) and brush each layer with sugar syrup to keep it moist (see page 12). Sandwich the layers together with cake filling, up to 0.5cm (just under ¼") deep.

2 Brush more sugar syrup over the surface of the cake before applying the crumb coat.

3 Using a large palette knife, spread an even layer of cake filling over the surface of the cake. Spread evenly to fill any gaps and create a smooth surface. If crumbs start to appear, add a little more filling and skim over the top surface.

4 Leave the cake to firm or refrigerate until you are ready to cover it with sugarpaste (see page 20). Prior to covering, rework the crumb coat with the palette knife to make it soft enough for the sugarpaste to stick, or brush a little sugar syrup over the surface.

Covering a Cake with Sugarpaste

All-in-one method (suitable for most cakes):

1 Knead the required amount of sugarpaste on a non-stick board dusted with icing sugar. Keep rotating the paste to create an even shape and ensure that it doesn't stick to the board. Do not turn the paste over as the icing sugar underneath may mark the surface.

2 Use a large rolling pin to roughly measure the cake covering area (i.e. across the top and down the sides) and roll out the paste to the required size with a thickness of around 3mm ($^1/_8$").

3 Lightly sprinkle the top of the sugarpaste with icing sugar to prevent sticking. To lift the paste, gently place the rolling pin in the centre and lightly fold the paste back over the rolling pin. This will prevent the paste from stretching and tearing. Lift carefully and position over the cake.

4 Smooth the covering down and around the cake with the palm of your hand, pressing gently around the sides to remove any air bubbles.

5 When you have smoothed over the top and sides of the cake, trim away the excess paste from around the base of the cake using a plain-bladed knife. Rub the surface gently with a cake smoother to remove any imperfections and achieve a smooth surface. After smoothing the sides, you may need to trim around the base once again to create a neat edge.

6 If you need to work on the sugarpaste while it is still soft, do this straight away. Otherwise, leave the sugarpaste for several hours as this will give you a firm surface on which to work.

tip

Occasionally, especially when covering unusual cake shapes, you may find you have a stubborn pleat in the sugarpaste. It is often quicker to pinch it together and cut away the spare paste than to stretch it out and smooth it over. To remove the cut line, press the join closed by pinching gently and then rub with your hands until the join is blended in. A little icing sugar on your fingers will help to remove the line completely.

Top and sides separately (suitable for cakes where sharp edges are required):

1 Roll out the sugarpaste as described in step 1 of the all-in-one method. This time, instead of rolling out the sugarpaste big enough to cover the whole cake, roll out a piece only the size of the area you wish to cover. Cut a neat shape, using a template if necessary or measuring carefully with a ruler.

2 Using a palette knife, carefully lift the paste to avoid tearing or distorting the shape and apply to the cake. Trim to size if necessary and smooth any joins closed with your fingertips. If you are making a very long piece (e.g. to go all the way around the sides of a cake), lightly dust the surface with icing sugar, roll up the paste and position the end against the cake before unrolling it around the sides.

3 Allow to firm for several hours, as above.

Covering a Cake Board (Drum)

1 Moisten the surface of the cake board slightly with a little cooled, boiled water using a pastry brush.

2 Knead the sugarpaste and roll out on a non-stick board dusted with icing sugar. Make sure the paste is big enough to cover the board and is no more than 2mm-3mm (just under 1/8") thick. When rolling out, move the paste around to prevent sticking but do not turn it over.

3 Carefully fold the sugarpaste over the rolling pin, lift the sugarpaste and position it on the cake board. Gently smooth over the top of the covered cake board with a cake smoother.

4 Hold the board underneath with one hand and, using a plain-bladed knife, trim away the excess sugarpaste from around the edge or, if you prefer a slightly rounded look, rub around the edge with a cake smoother until the paste becomes thin and tears away easily.

5 To finish the board, you will need to trim the edge with co-ordinating 15mm-width ribbon (this is slightly deeper than the cake board to allow for the depth of the sugarpaste covering). Measure the length needed to go around the board and allow an extra 2cm (¾") or so to overlap at the back.

6 Rub a non-toxic, solid glue stick around the cake board edge, taking care not to touch the sugarpaste covering. If you prefer, double-sided tape can be used. Starting at the back of the cake, stick the ribbon around the cake board edge, running your finger along the bottom to keep the ribbon straight. Overlap the ribbon slightly and cut off the excess at the join. Ensure the join is positioned at the back of the cake.

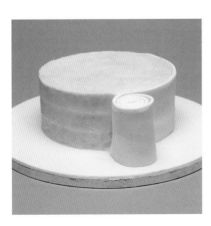

Dowelling a Cake

If a cake has two or more tiers or is particularly tall, you will need to dowel the lower tiers after they have been coated to make sure that the cakes stack evenly and are well-supported and balanced.

1 Make a template of the cake top from greaseproof paper and fold in half twice to find the centre. Draw a circle on the paper around the central point – the circle must fit within the size and shape of the tier that will be placed on top in order to support it. Mark the dowel points evenly around the circle – the number of dowels you need will depend on the size of the cake and number of tiers (see each project for details).

2 Using the template and a pointed tool (or the tip of a knife), mark the position of the dowels on the cake. Insert the plastic dowels into the cake, ensuring that they are vertical and go all the way down to the cake board. Using a pencil, mark each dowel just above the level of

the sugarpaste covering, making sure the pencil does not touch the sugarpaste itself. Alternatively, score each dowel carefully with a knife.

3 Remove the dowels, place them on a work surface and line up the bottom of each. The markings may vary, so find the lowest mark and score all the dowels at this point with a craft knife (this ensures the cake stands upright, has no gaps and does not lean). Snap each dowel to size (if using plastic dowels, otherwise cut to size) and then insert them back into the holes in the cake; they should each sit level with the cake top (or just below it if the cake is uneven).

Covering Mini Cakes with Sugarpaste

Mini cakes are popular at any celebration, either alongside a larger cake or instead of one, and look extremely pretty and stylish when presented well. Suggested designs are given alongside each project which co-ordinate with the style of the main cake, so you can use this as inspiration or create your own designs.

Mini cakes can be made in several different shapes, including square and round. Although you can cut these from sheet cakes using good quality, deep cutters, I recommend the mini cake bakeware and liners by Squires Kitchen, available from sugarcraft stockists (see page 112). These cake pans are purpose-made which makes the job easier, eliminates wastage and guarantees the correct shape and size, no matter how many cakes are required. Silicone bakeware is useful for unusual shapes such as spheres and domes as the cakes can be turned out easily.

Important Note: Make sure the dowels and any other inedible items on the cake are removed before serving.

Using Colour

Food colourings are available as liquids, paints, pastes and dusts (also known as powders). Liquid colours and paints are generally used for painting onto sugar; pastes are ideal for colouring roll-out icings (such as sugarpaste and modelling paste) and royal icing; and dusts can be brushed onto the surface of sugar pieces or mixed with clear alcohol to make a quick-drying paint.

1 If required, cut one or two layers in the cake, depending on the size and shape. For ball shapes, sandwich the two halves together. Layer and crumb-coat the cake with filling (see recipes on pages 12 to 13).

2 Roll the sugarpaste a little thinner than you would for a large cake – around 2mm (under $^1/_8$") deep – then cover in the usual way (pages 20 to 21). Use a cake smoother to press the top and sides smooth.

3 Trim the paste neatly around the base of the cake. You can speed this up by using a hollow cutter the same shape and slightly larger than the mini cake to cut around the base cleanly and neatly. Simply move the cutter down over the

mini cake, press it into the excess paste around the base and then remove.

4 Place each mini cake on a small cake card or piece of greaseproof paper cut to size to protect and seal the cake and then decorate as required.

Squires Kitchen makes a huge range of colours for cake and food decoration. All of their colours are edible, light-fast, tartrazine-free and glycerine-free and are readily available from Squires Kitchen (see page 112) or your local stockist. If you are not using ready-coloured pastes and icings, you will need to colour them at least two hours before starting a project to allow the colour to develop.

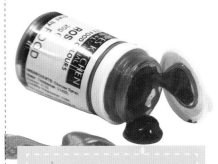

> ### tip
>
> Mini cakes make a great party bag filler as an alternative to the traditional slice of cake. Decorate as required, then place in small boxes or cellophane bags tied with co-ordinating ribbon.

> ### tip
>
> Paste food colours are concentrated, so only add a tiny amount of paste food colour at a time using a cocktail stick until the desired colour is achieved. Blend the colour into the paste by kneading well and allow to 'rest' in an airtight food-grade polythene bag for a couple of hours before use.

basic techniques 23

wash day

This design came to mind first in pale blue to depict a sky, teamed with brightly coloured clothing, but the soft hues of pink and pale chocolate brown won over, making a stylish and fashionable alternative.

Edibles

2 x 15cm (6") round cakes, each 8cm (3") depth (see recipes on pages 6 to 9)

10cm (4") round cake, 8cm (3") depth (see recipes on pages 6 to 9)

50g (1¾oz) cake truffle for each wash basket (see recipe on page 11)

450g (1lb) cake filling/crumb coat (see recipes on pages 12 to 13)

Sugarpaste (rolled fondant):

315g (11oz) pink/beige (coloured with pink with a touch of brown)

900g (2lb) beige (coloured with a touch of brown)

30g (1oz) pale pink

Modelling paste:

30g (1oz) mid-beige

10g (¼oz) brown

5g (just under ¼oz) dark pink

45g (1½oz) pale brown

30g (1oz) pale pink

15g (½oz) soft beige

30g (1oz) white

45g (1½oz) royal icing

Paste or liquid food colours: black, brown, pink (SK)

Edible glue (see recipe on page 15) (SK)

Equipment

Basic equipment (see pages 16 to 18)

30cm (12") round cake board

2 x 12cm (5") and 1 x 8cm (3") round cake cards

6 x food-safe plastic dowels

Fine and medium paintbrushes (SK)

Parchment/greaseproof paper

Template (see page 111)

Small blossom cutter

1cm (³/₈") circle cutter

Set of tiny miniature cutters: flowers and hearts

Piping nozzles (tips): nos. 1, 1.5, 4 (PME)

A few cocktail sticks

Cake Board

1 Knead the pink/beige sugarpaste until it is soft and pliable. Sprinkle the work surface with icing sugar, rub a little onto the top of the sugarpaste and then roll out, moving the paste around to prevent sticking after each roll, until you have a thickness of 2-3mm (¹/₈") and the paste is large enough to cover the cake board.

2 Moisten the cake board with a little cooled, boiled water or edible glue and then lift and position the sugarpaste onto the board. Smooth the surface with a cake smoother, trim the excess from around the edge and then set aside to dry.

Cake

3 Trim the crust from each cake and level the tops, reserving the trimmings. Cut layers in each cake and then sandwich them back together with cake filling, keeping each cake separate at this stage. Position all of the cakes on their respective cake cards.

4 As the bottom tier is double height the lower part needs to be dowelled to prevent any distortion. Push three dowels down through the centre of one of the larger cakes, right down to the board the cake is sitting on. Make a small mark on each dowel level with the top of the cake and then remove. Cut each dowel to the lowest mark to ensure that subsequent tiers will still sit straight.

5 Place the second 15cm (6") round cake on top of the dowelled cake, securing with a spread of cake filling on the top. Spread the whole cake surface with cake filling as a crumb coat to seal the cake and help the sugarpaste stick. The cake should now measure around 14cm (5½") in height. Spread a covering of filling over the smaller cake in the same way and set aside.

6 Roll out 650g (1lb 7oz) of beige sugarpaste and cover the bottom cake completely, smoothing down and around the shape. Smooth the surface with a cake smoother and then trim away the excess paste from around the base. Carefully lift

and position the cake in the centre of the cake board, securing around the edge with a little edible glue.

7 Cover the smaller cake with sugarpaste as before. Dowel the top part of the base cake, cutting the dowels level with the sugarpaste covering, then position the smaller cake on top, securing with edible glue as before.

Washing Basket

8 Mix some cake filling and some of the cake crumbs together to make a truffle (see page 11). To make the basket shape, roll 50g (1¾oz) of the cake truffle into a ball then roll gently at the bottom to narrow slightly, pressing down at the opposite end to flatten. Place a small circle of parchment/greaseproof paper on the underside and then refrigerate for five minutes to allow the texture to firm up.

9 Brush a little cake filling over the surface to help the sugarpaste stick. Thinly roll out the pale pink sugarpaste and cover

the basket completely, smoothing down and around the shape. Trim away the excess from around the base. Indent two lines into the surface using the back of the knife then set aside.

Washing Line

10 Thinly roll out the pale brown modelling paste and cut strips to make the washing line poles. Cut three poles for the bottom tier measuring 11cm (4¼") in height and three for the top tier measuring 7.5cm (3"). Carefully stick them in position evenly spaced around the cake and add a small, flattened ball to the top of each. Score lines between each pole for the washing line using the tip of a knife.

Mum-to-be

11 Make the mum-to-be using modelling paste and following the template. Model her trousers first using 10g (¼oz) of pale brown: roll into a sausage shape, place on the template and then stretch and

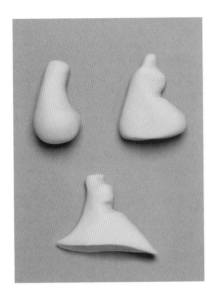

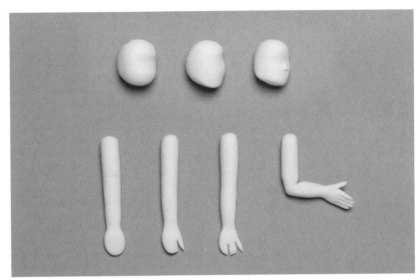

smooth until the paste fills the outline. To make the shoe, roll a small ball of pale pink into a sausage shape and indent the centre slightly by rolling back and forth. Stick the shoe in position with the trousers on the top then secure to the cake with edible glue.

12 Roll a teardrop shape for her belly using just under half of the soft beige modelling paste and stick in position with a minute ball for a belly button. Using 5g (just under ¼oz) of pale pink, model her top. Stick both to the cake.

13 To make an arm, roll 2g (pinch) of soft beige modelling paste into a sausage shape and round off one end for the hand. Press down on the hand to flatten slightly and pinch gently on either side to lengthen. Make a cut for the thumb no further than halfway between the top of the hand and the wrist and then make three further cuts along the top to separate the fingers. Bend the arm at the elbow by pushing in and then pinching out at the back.

14 Make a tiny neck using soft beige modelling paste. Split the remaining soft beige in half and use one half for the head. Roll this into a ball and roll over the work surface slightly to flatten the facial area. Indent the eye area with a paintbrush handle. Stroke the mouth area downwards and pinch the resulting excess paste on either side to shape a chin. Stick in position and add a tiny teardrop-shaped nose.

15 Add a flattened teardrop of brown modelling paste for her hair and cut at the front to create curls. Stick a small piece onto the opposite side, flicking up into a curl at the bottom. Dilute pink and black food colouring with cooled, boiled water or use liquid colouring to paint the eyes and mouth using the fine paintbrush.

Baby Clothes

16 **Tops:** Thinly roll out the coloured modelling paste and cut out a square or oblong, depending on the shape of the top. Cut a semicircle from the top using

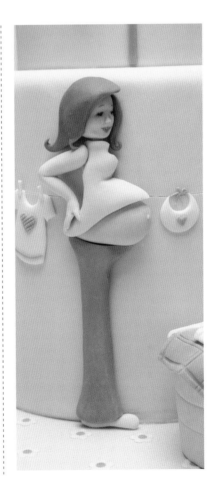

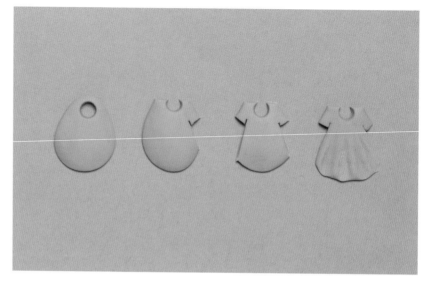

a small circle cutter and then cut either side at an angle to create the outside of each sleeve. Cut straight down on either side, up to just under the arm, then cut the bottom of each sleeve straight.

17 Dresses: Cut out as for a top but roll a paintbrush handle across the bottom part to stretch the paste and create frills.

18 Dungarees: Cut an oblong shape, take out a small square or semicircle from the top and then cut at the bottom to separate the legs. Smooth around the shape to soften the hard edges and then add a small circular pocket on the front, opening it up at the top a little.

19 All-in-one sleep suit: Cut out a small oblong shape of modelling paste then cut either side for the sleeves and make a small cut at the bottom to separate the legs. Pinch up the feet. Mark a line down the centre followed by poppers using the tip of a cocktail stick. Indent patterns and mark cuffs. Add a

tiny collar to the top cut from the small circle cutter with a small piece cut out at the front.

20 Socks: Roll pea-sized pieces of modelling paste into small sausage shapes and bend round, smoothing out the foot area. Cut the top of each sock straight.

21 Leggings: Make leggings from a small sausage of modelling paste. Press down to flatten, cut down the centre to separate the legs and pinch up at the bottom to make the feet.

22 Baby blankets: Cut different sized squares from thinly rolled paste. Indent lines and dots using the back of a knife and a cocktail stick or add flower shapes, stripes or teddy bears (see below).

Toys

23 Teddy bear: To make the teddy bear, roll a small teardrop shape for a tummy and press down to flatten. Stick two small

oval shapes at the bottom for feet and add two small sausage-shaped arms. Roll a ball for his head and a smaller one for the muzzle, indenting the top with the tip of a knife. Stick two ears on top, both indented with the end of a paintbrush. Add a tiny oval-shaped nose and thinly roll out and cut two small, black circles for eyes using a 1.5 piping nozzle.

24 **Rabbit:** Make the rabbit as for the teddy bear and add a tiny teardrop patch to his tummy. Make his ears from tapering sausage shapes, indent both slightly and fill with pink. Add a pink nose.

25 **Birds:** To make a bird, roll a small teardrop shape for the body and cut into the point to make the tail feathers. Roll two tiny teardrop shapes for wings, then flatten and cut feathers along the bottom of each. For the head, roll a small ball and add a pink teardrop shape onto the face for a beak, using a pair of fine scissors to snip the beak open. Make two eyes with the piping nozzle as before.

Detailing

26 To make buttons for the dress roll two tiny ball shapes and indent the centre of each with the end of a paintbrush. Stick in position and then make two holes in the centre using the tip of a cocktail stick.

27 Add different shapes and patterns to the clothing using the heart and flower cutters and cut out large dots using the piping nozzles. Divide the royal icing into three and colour pale brown, pale pink and dark pink. Place each colour into a piping back with a no. 1 nozzle and pipe ribbons, lines and polka dots onto the clothes.

28 To decorate the cake board, thinly roll out some pale pink modelling paste and cut out flower shapes using the medium blossom cutter. Roll out the pale brown paste and cut small circles for the centre of each using a no. 4 piping nozzle.

29 Thinly roll out the remaining soft beige modelling paste and cut minute strips for the pegs. Stick in position using a little edible glue.

mini teddy parcels

Extra/alternative requirements for each parcel:

Edibles

6cm (2½") square cake, 4cm (1½") height

A little cake filling (see recipes on pages 12 to 13)

Sugarpaste (rolled fondant):

15g (½oz) cream or pale pink (for the top)

75g (2½oz) brown

Modelling paste:

10g (¼oz) (for the bear)

Equipment

6cm (2½") square cake cards

6cm (2½") square cutter (optional)

30cm (12") x 15mm width ribbon: pale pink

1 Place each cake onto a cake card. Split and fill with one layer of cake filling and then spread a crumb coat over the surface to seal the cake and help the sugarpaste stick.

2 Cover the top of each cake with a layer of sugarpaste in your chosen colour (unless you're making the tartan effect, see below) then indent the pattern using a ruler or score with a knife. Add a modelled bear on the top.

3 To create the tartan pattern, thinly roll out the base colour, in this case pale pink. Thinly roll out two more colours, such as pale brown and white, and cut into strips of different widths. As these strips will be rolled into the first paste they need to be as thin as possible otherwise the lines will distort. Stick the brown strips in position first and then the white. Press down gently

to ensure the lines are secure and then gently roll over the surface with a rolling pin until the surface is completely smooth and the pattern is inlayed. Add a modelled bear as before.

4 Roll out some brown sugarpaste and cut out four 6cm (2½") squares, turning out the corners of each slightly. You can either use a square cutter or measure each square carefully with a ruler. Attach these to the sides of the cake then tie with 15mm pale pink ribbon.

tip

For a fun alternative, these cakes can be decorated with different baby clothes made from modelling paste.

truffle washing baskets

These little baskets also work well as individual mini cakes, filled with cake truffle mixture. Make in the same way as for the basket with the main cake.

stork delivery

I love the tale of storks delivering babies but to design a cake with a flying bird holding something is tricky, especially if you want maximum impact with minimum work. Here the simple but effective modelled figures are supported securely against the cake. Hmmm, on reflection… This is how babies are delivered, right?

Edibles

20cm (8") round cake, 8cm (3") depth
(see recipes on pages 6 to 9)

15cm (6") round cake, 8cm (3") depth
(see recipes on pages 6 to 9)

1 x 10cm (4") round cake, 6cm (2½")
depth (see recipes on pages 6 to 9)

450g (1lb) cake filling/crumb coat (see
recipes on pages 12 to 13)

Sugarpaste (rolled fondant):
  1.6kg (3lb 8½oz) white

Modelling paste:
  tiny piece black
  5g (just under ¼oz) pale yellow
  10g (⅓oz) soft beige
  120g (4¼oz) white
20g (¾oz) royal icing
Paste food colour: blue (SK)
Dust food colour: pink (SK)
Edible glue (see recipe on page 15)
35ml (2tbsp) cooled, boiled water

Equipment

Basic equipment (see pages 16 to 18)

30cm (12") round cake board

7.5cm (3"), 13cm (5") and 18cm (7")
round cake cards

6 x food-safe plastic dowels

Large pastry brush

Small piece of folded card

Kitchen paper

Piping nozzle (tip): no. 16 (PME) or
drinking straw

Fine and medium paintbrushes (SK)

Cake Board

1 Knead 315g (11oz) of white sugarpaste until soft and pliable. Sprinkle the work surface with icing sugar, rub a little onto the top of the sugarpaste and then roll out, moving the paste around to prevent sticking after each roll, until you have a thickness of 2-3mm (⅛") and the paste is large enough to cover the cake board.

2 Moisten the cake board with a little cooled, boiled water or edible glue and then lift and position the sugarpaste onto the board. Smooth the surface with a cake smoother, trim the excess from around the edge and then set aside to dry.

Cake

3 Trim the crust from each cake and level the tops. To ensure the cakes are completely level and flat on the top, turn each cake over and use the base as the top. Cut layers in each cake and sandwich back together using cake filling; keep each cake separate at this stage. Place the cakes on their respective, slightly smaller cake cards and then spread a layer of cake filling over the surface of each one to seal the cake and help the sugarpaste stick.

4 To cover the largest cake, roll out 800g (1lb 12oz) of white sugarpaste and cover the cake completely, smoothing around the cake, stretching out any pleats and smoothing downwards. Cut away the

excess from around the base and smooth the surface with a cake smoother. Place this cake centrally on the cake board and use a dab of royal icing underneath to secure it in place. Cover the two remaining cakes in the same way using the remaining white sugarpaste.

5 To dowel the base cake, push three dowels down through the centre of the cake, keeping them evenly spaced and well within a 13cm (5") diameter. Mark each one level with the top of the sugarpaste by scoring gently and then remove from the cake. Place the three dowels down on the work surface together so that they are level at the bottom and check the marks are in the same position. If they are not this means your cake is not completely level. To ensure the finished cake does not lean, cut each dowel at the lowest mark and insert back into the cake. Dowel the middle tier in the same way, keeping the dowels well within an 8cm (3") diameter.

6 Position the middle tier and top tier on top of the larger cake, securing with a tiny

dab of royal icing. Dilute a little blue paste food colour with cooled, boiled water and use a large pastry brush to paint the surface of the cake. Create a simple sky effect with lines and streaks, deepening the colour around the bottom half.

Clouds

7 Using the white sugarpaste trimmings, model all the different sized clouds. To make a cloud, first roll an oval shape and press down with a cake smoother to flatten it slightly. To shape, fold a small piece of card in half and then press the fold around the outside edge of the cloud, allowing the card to open slightly. Smooth with your fingertips to round off further. Make all the remaining clouds and stick these in position with a little edible glue.

Stork

8 Roll 45g (1½oz) of white modelling paste into a sausage shape measuring

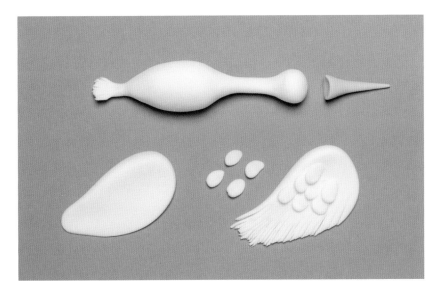
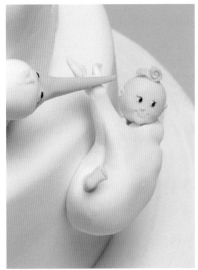

7cm (2¾"). Pinch near one end to round off the head and roll down further to create the long neck. Roll the opposite end to narrow it further and then smooth down at the tip.

9 Cut the tail feathers using a knife. Secure the body in position against the cake and cloud using a dab of royal icing and wedge a small piece of rolled up kitchen paper underneath to hold it in place until completely dry.

10 To make the wings, split 30g (1oz) of white modelling paste in half and roll each piece into a teardrop shape. Roll out to flatten, keeping the rounded end slightly thicker. Cut feathers along the bottom of each wing on opposite sides and then stick small, flattened balls of sugarpaste over the surface using a little edible glue, smoothing down the paste on one side of each with your fingertip to create feathers. Set aside the finished wings to firm slightly and then secure in place with royal icing, as before.

11 To make the beak, roll just over half of the yellow modelling paste into a long teardrop shape and cut the rounded end straight. Smooth in the centre of the cut using your fingertip to widen it and then set aside to firm slightly before sticking in position.

12 For the stork's legs, first put aside a pea-sized piece of yellow for the baby's hair later and then split the remainder in half. To make a leg, roll a thin sausage shape and bend one end round for the foot. Roll gently to narrow the ankle and round off the heel. Pinch either side of the foot to narrow it and then cut twice into the end. To bend, pinch out the joint at the back and push in halfway. Make the second leg and then stick each one in position.

13 Stick the beak in position and indent two tiny nostrils with the tip of a cocktail stick. Add two tiny oval-shaped white eyes with slightly smaller black pupils. Stick two tiny teardrops of white onto the top of the head for the feathers.

Sling

14 First set aside 5g (just under ¼oz) of white modelling paste for later and then roll the remainder into a rounded teardrop shape to make the sling. Pinch up the point to elongate it and then indent the openings on either side using a paintbrush handle, making an area for the baby's body and leg. Smooth some fabric-effect ripples with your fingertip. Stick the sling onto the cake with royal icing and support as before.

Baby

15 Put a pea-sized piece of soft beige modelling paste into the sling for the baby's body. To make the head, roll 5g (just under ¼oz) into a ball and flatten the face slightly. Indent the smile by pushing in with the tip of a no. 16 nozzle or drinking straw to mark a semi-circle, then add dimples using a cocktail stick.

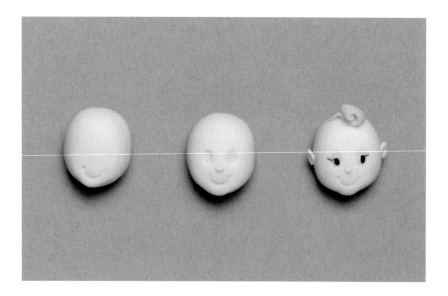

16 Roll a tiny, oval-shaped nose and two slightly larger oval shapes for ears, then indent the centre of the ears using the end of a paintbrush. Make the eyes as before and edge the top of each with a minute sausage of black paste for the eyelashes. Brush a little pink dust colour over the baby's cheeks and then stick the head in position using a dab of royal icing. For the baby curl, roll the remaining pale yellow paste into a sausage, flatten slightly and gently roll up. Stick the features in position with a dab of edible glue.

17 Roll the remaining soft beige modelling paste into a tiny sausage for the leg and bend one end round to make the foot. Roll gently to narrow at the ankle and pinch to shape the heel. Make tiny cuts for toes and then smooth round the smaller toes to curl them slightly. Stick the leg in position.

18 At the side of the stork's beak, add a ball for the knot of the sling. Make two teardrop shapes for the ends on either side of the knot and indent slightly with a paintbrush.

tip

Instead of using minute pieces of black paste, you can paint the eyes and eyelashes with diluted black food colour using an extra-fine paintbrush if you find it easier.

Extra/alternative requirements for each cake:

Edibles

6cm (2½") half-sphere cake baked in heat-resistant silicone bowls or trays, filled

A little cake filling, jam or sugar syrup (see recipes on pages 12 to 13)

Sugarpaste (rolled fondant):

45g (1½oz) pale blue, pale yellow or pale blue

Equipment

10cm (4") circle cutter (optional)

New plastic pan scourer or wicker texture mat/roller

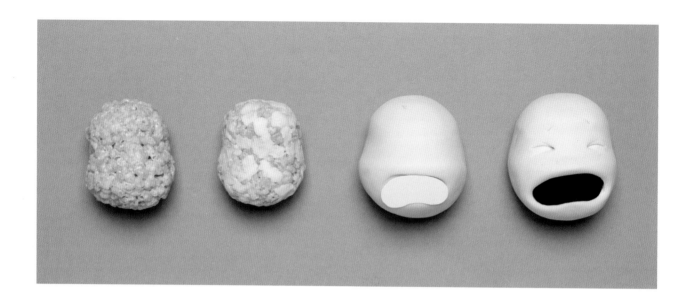

differently to ensure the second tier sits straight. Insert the dowels back into the cake.

6 Using the remaining white sugarpaste, cover the smaller cake as before and then position it centrally on top the larger cake, securing with a little edible glue. Thinly roll out some blue modelling paste and cut out wavy shapes for the puddles. Stick them around the base of both cakes with edible glue. Save a little blue modelling paste for the babies' tears later.

Heads

7 For each baby head you will need 25g (just over ¾oz) of marshmallow rice cereal mixture. Roll each portion into a ball whilst the mixture is still warm (see instructions on page 10) and indent the eye area slightly by rolling a rolling pin from side to side across the surface, just above halfway. Push a lolly stick 4cm (1½") into the base to make a hole and then remove. Make three heads altogether then leave to set for around ten minutes. When firm, fill any uneven areas with small pieces of soft beige sugarpaste.

8 To cover each head, roll out 50g (1¾oz) of soft beige sugarpaste and cover the shape completely. Smooth around the facial area first and then close the join at the back as near to the bottom as possible using a little edible glue. Cut away any excess paste and then rub the join gently to remove it completely. Cover the remaining two heads in the same way. Smooth over the surface to remove any imperfections.

9 Using the template, cut out the open mouth shape for two babies and fill with thinly rolled black modelling paste. Mark the closed eyes using the flat tip of a knife and then cut an upward curve for the scrunched up eye. Mark eyebrows using the tip of the knife.

10 For the sad baby, first indent the downturned mouth by pressing in with a circle cutter and smoothing the cut with a damp paintbrush. Press the paste underneath to push up the bottom lip and smooth again with the paintbrush. Indent the eyes using a bone or ball tool.

11 Stick small oval shapes onto each face for their noses and indent nostrils using the end of a paintbrush or pointed modelling tool. To make the ears, roll small oval shapes, indent the centre using the bone or ball tool and stick in position on the sides of the head, level with the nose.

12 Stick two small, white oval-shaped eyes onto the sad baby along with two smaller black ovals for pupils. Mark the closed eyes on the other two babies with the tip of a knife. Edge all eyes with a minute sausage of black paste for

tip

If you prefer, the eyelashes can be painted with either diluted black paste food colour or black liquid food colouring. Use the fine paintbrush and paint a very thin line. If you make a mistake the black colour can be removed using a clean, damp paintbrush.

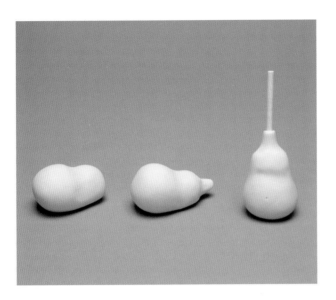

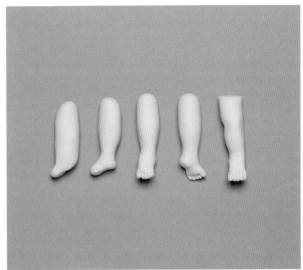

eyelashes. Paint a tiny highlight on the sad baby's eyes to one side using white paste food colour and a very fine paintbrush.

13 For the tonsils, roll two tiny sausages of red paste, round off each end then bend round and press each end flat. Cut tiny squares of white for the teeth. Stick the tonsils and teeth into the mouth with edible glue.

14 Dust pink dust colour liberally over their cheeks using a dry, flat paintbrush. Roll teardrop shapes of pale blue paste for the tears and 'fill' the sad baby's eyes with small pieces, smoothing them down gently.

Bodies

15 For each body you will need 45g (1½oz) of soft beige modelling paste. Roll the paste into a rounded teardrop shape and gently pinch a neck at the narrow end. Make a hole in the neck using a cocktail stick and twist it around to open up the hole further until it is large enough for the lolly stick. Moisten the lolly stick with

edible glue and then push it down into the body, leaving some protruding to support the head later. Stroke the paste a third of the way down to round off the tummy area and indent the belly button using a cocktail stick.

Legs

16 Use 15g (½oz) of soft beige modelling paste to make each pair of legs. To make a leg, roll a sausage shape measuring no more than 4cm (1½") in length. Bend one end round for the foot and roll at the ankle to round off the heel and shape the leg. Squeeze the foot on either side to lengthen and narrow it slightly.

17 Cut the big toe first, pull out and press flat then round off the edges slightly and push back in. Stroke the remaining toe area flat and cut the rest of the toes level with the big toe. Cut four further toes and gently round off each one. Pinch the knee halfway between the ankle and top of the leg and push in at the back to bend it slightly. Roll a paintbrush handle or pointed

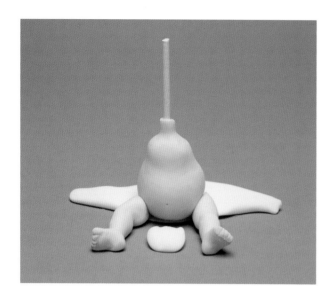

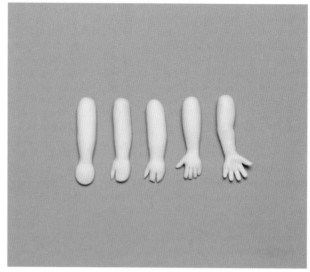

modelling tool over the ankle area at the front to indent the shape. The whole leg from top to heel should measure around 5cm (2") in length. Make five more legs, left and right, and then set aside to dry.

Nappy

18 Roll 20g (¾oz) of white modelling paste into a sausage shape and then roll each end to narrow slightly. Flatten the shape with a rolling pin until it measures 13cm (5") in length. Position a baby's body down onto it with two legs at the front, moisten either side of the nappy with edible glue and then wrap the paste around the body and over the legs. Add a small oval shape of white to the centre for the knot and indent slightly to create pleats.

Arms

19 These will need an internal support so gently push a lolly stick into either side of both screaming babies, leaving around 3cm (1¼") protruding. To make an arm, split the remaining soft beige modelling paste into six equally sized pieces. Roll one piece into a sausage shape measuring 4cm (1½") in length. Roll gently at one end to round off the hand and press down to flatten slightly. Make a cut on one side for the thumb and then three slightly shorter cuts along the top for the fingers. Gently roll each finger to round off the edges.

20 Pinch halfway between the wrist and the top of the arm to indent the elbow. Moisten the lolly stick with a little edible glue. Make a hole in the arm using a cocktail stick and twist it around to make it larger so the arm fits over the lolly stick, then secure the arm in place. Make the remaining left and right arms for all the babies. For the sad baby, gently bend the hand into the pose and support with kitchen paper until dry. Moisten all the arms at the joins with edible glue and gently rub in a circular motion to blend the paste and remove the joins completely.

Hair

21 Push a head down onto each body and secure with a little edible glue. Roll two tiny sausages of brown modelling paste for the brown haired baby and stick in place. Roll a small curl for the middle baby using a pea-sized amount of pale yellow paste. For the sad baby, stick a small teardrop of yellow on top of the head and smooth into the surface using a damp paintbrush. Add a tiny curl on the forehead.

Bow

22 To make the bow, roll two flattened, tapering sausages of pink, loop them around and secure with edible glue. Add a small ball of pink to the hair and then stick the loops on either side. Add a tiny teardrop of yellow to the top.

mini nappy bags

Extra/alternative requirements for each bag:

Materials

7cm x 5cm (2¾" x 2") oblong cakes, 2.5cm depth, layered with a little filling (see recipes on pages 12 to 13)

Sugarpaste (rolled fondant):

90g (3oz) pale blue, pale yellow or white

1   To cover, thinly roll out 90g (3oz) of sugarpaste and cut an oblong measuring 14cm x 18cm (5½" x 7"). Place the cake down onto the bottom half (see step picture) and fold over the opposite sides. Fold up the bottom, secure to the cake with edible glue, then fold over the top make the flap opening.

2   Thinly roll out the sugarpaste trimmings and cut out pockets and straps to decorate the bag. You can then model tiny bottles, rubber ducks or teddies from the trimmings to go on the bag or in the pockets.

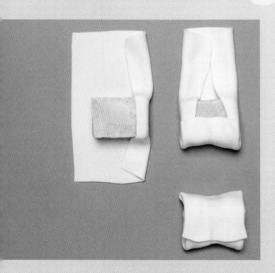

tip

These can be cut from any size cake depending on how many you need to make. I used a 7cm x 5cm (2¾" x 2") oblong shape for each with a 2.5cm (1") depth, so out of a 30cm (12") square cake 2.5cm (1") deep you can make 24 of these.

mini faces

To make mini baby faces, cover 7cm (2¾")
dome-shaped cakes with 35g (1¼oz)
of soft beige sugarpaste and make the
features following the instructions for the
babies on the main cake. Model a dummy
from sugarpaste and use a small ball of
modelling paste for the base. Place each
cake onto a small, round cake card or a
circle of greaseproof paper.

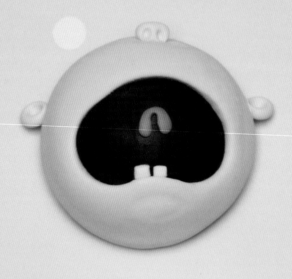

mini dummy (pacifier) cakes

Extra/alternative requirements for each dummy:

Edibles

7cm (2¾") dome-shaped cake (baked in an ovenproof silicone bowl or mould)

A little cake filling (see recipe on pages 12 to 13)

Sugarpaste:

35g (1¼oz) in your choice of colours

Modelling paste:

50g (1¾oz)

10g (¼oz) soft beige

Paste or liquid food colour: black (SK) (optional)

1 Level the top of the dome-shaped cake and then spread some cake filling over the surface to help the sugarpaste stick. Roll out 35g (1¼oz) of sugarpaste and cover the domed part of the cake, leaving the top with just a covering of cake filling.

2 To make the top part of the dummy, thickly roll out 45g (1½oz) of modelling paste into an 8cm (3") circle. Push in at the top to create an indent and then smooth around the edge with your fingers to round off. Leave to dry flat before positioning on the cake. Make a small sausage of the same colour, curl it around for the handle and stick it in place with edible glue. For extra decoration, paint a dotty pattern using diluted paste food colour or liquid colour.

3 Take a small piece of soft beige modelling paste, roll a rounded teardrop for the sucker and cut off the point. Leave to firm slightly before sticking in position.

pea in a pod

The thought of slicing up this cake seemed a bit bizarre but the design in my head was so cute I compromised a little by making the head with marshmallow rice cereal. Although a tasty treat in itself, I was a little happier that at least this wouldn't be ceremoniously cut up during serving!

Edibles

2 x 15cm (6") bowl-shaped cakes (see recipes on pages 6 to 9)

400g (14oz) cake filling/crumb coat (see recipes on pages 12 to 13)

225g (8oz) marshmallow rice cereal (see recipe on page 10)

Sugarpaste (rolled fondant):

  800g (1lb 12oz) soft beige

  315g (11oz) white

Modelling paste:

  2g (pinch) black

  2g (pinch) brown

  500g (1lb 1¾oz) green

  145g (5oz) soft beige

Edible glue (see recipe on page 15) (SK)

Paste food colour: white (SK)

Dust food colour: pale pink (SK)

Equipment

Basic equipment (see pages 16 to 18)

30cm (12") round cake board

Food-safe plastic cake dowel

Fine and medium paintbrushes (SK)

A few cocktail sticks

Cake Board

1 Knead the white sugarpaste until it is soft and pliable. Sprinkle the work surface with icing sugar, rub a little onto the top of the sugarpaste and then roll out, moving the paste around to prevent sticking after each roll, until you have a thickness of 2-3mm (⅛") and the paste is large enough to cover the cake board.

2 Moisten the cake board with a little cooled, boiled water or edible glue and then lift and position the sugarpaste onto the board. Smooth the surface with a cake smoother, trim the excess from around the edge and then set aside to dry.

Baby's Head

3 Make the marshmallow rice cereal following the recipe. Whilst the mixture is still warm, mould into an oval shape measuring 10cm x 13cm (4" x 5"). Place this down on the work surface and roll back and forth gently so one side flattens slightly; this area will be the baby's face. To make a hole for the dowel that will support the head on the body, push a dowel into the bottom and up to midway through the shape whilst the mixture is still a little soft. Remove the dowel and set aside to firm.

4 Once the head has set, use small pieces of soft beige sugarpaste to fill in any uneven areas and create a smooth surface ready for the sugarpaste covering. To pad out the mouth area, roll 2g (pinch) of soft beige sugarpaste into an oval shape and stick this onto the bottom half of the face using edible glue.

tip

Ganache is a good covering for marshmallow rice cereal as it can be spread easily to create a smooth surface prior to covering and will set quickly if placed in the refrigerator.

5 Brush the surface with a little edible glue. Roll out 175g (6oz) of soft beige sugarpaste and use this to cover the face and bottom half of the head. To remove the ridge, smooth the edge until it is level with the surface. Smooth around the mouth and indent the centre using the back of a knife, pushing the tip in at each corner to dimple. Smooth the surface and around the padding using a damp paintbrush, shaping the lips carefully.

6 Add a small, oval-shaped nose using the paste trimmings and mark each nostril with the end of a paintbrush. Push into each eye area with your fingertips to make the eye sockets and smooth around the edge of each one. Set aside until later.

Body

7 Trim the crust from each cake and level the tops. Cut a layer in each cake and then place one cake on top of the other to form a ball shape. Trim around the top half of the cake to make it narrower for the chest and shoulder area. Sandwich the layers together with cake filling and then spread a thin layer over the surface of the cake to help the sugarpaste stick.

8 Roll out 625g (1lb 6oz) of soft beige sugarpaste and cover the cake completely, smoothing the paste down and around the shape. Stretch out the pleats around the bottom and smooth downwards again, trimming away excess.

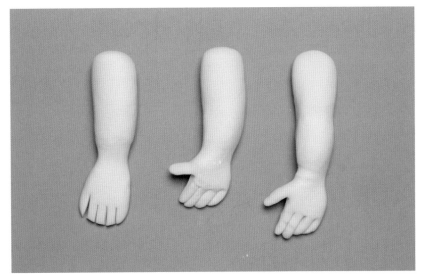

Smooth with a cake smoother or use a small ball of sugarpaste dusted with icing sugar and rub this over the surface of the cake in a circular motion to smooth out any dimples. Mark the belly button indentation using your fingertip.

9   Lift the cake carefully and stick it onto the centre of the cake board using a little edible glue. Push the dowel down through the body, leaving some protruding at the top, then push the head down over the dowel until the head sits comfortably on top of the body.

10   The pod is made in two halves so first split 300g (10½oz) of green modelling paste in half and set one piece aside to make the hat later. Roll the first piece into a sausage shape and taper at both ends. Roll over the surface with the rolling pin, stretching the paste until it measures around 30cm (12") in length and 9cm (3½") at the deepest point in the centre, keeping an even shape. If it starts to distort then gently push the paste back and roll again. Smooth around the edge to round off and repeat on the opposite side.

11   Moisten around the bottom half of the baby's body with edible glue and leave to become tacky for one to two minutes (this ensures the sides will stick properly when applied). Smooth the sides in position against the tacky glue and stick the two opposite ends together.

Arms

12   Split the soft beige modelling paste in half for the arms. To make an arm, first roll the paste into a smooth, blemish-free ball then roll into a short sausage shape and round off one end for the hand. Smooth the hand down and narrow slightly on either side.

13   Make a cut for the thumb first, no further than halfway from the top to the wrist. Ensure the cut is straight, leaving a straight edge from which to cut all the fingers. Cut in the centre first and then once more on either side, making the cuts slightly shorter than for the thumb.

14   Roll each finger and thumb gently to round off the edges and lengthen slightly, rolling deeper at the knuckle to indent the paste. Mark the fingernails by indenting with the handle of a paintbrush. Push the thumb down towards the palm to shape the hand and then roll the paintbrush handle across the top of the wrist to indent.

15   For each elbow, push in gently halfway between the wrist and the shoulder, pinch the paste out at the back and then smooth the shoulder down slightly. Moisten the body with edible glue and leave to become tacky as before, then stick the arms in position, holding for a few moments until secure.

Eyes

16   Depending on how deep you've pushed in to make the eye sockets, roll two small oval shapes of white modelling paste and fill the sockets to make the eyes. Add two flattened circles of brown to the lower half of each eye followed by

mini pea cakes

smaller black circles for pupils. Roll minute black eyelashes using black modelling paste. Using the fine paintbrush and white paste food colour, paint a tiny highlight in exactly the same position on each eye.

Hat

17 Moisten around the top half of the head with edible glue. Roll out the remaining green paste into an oval shape and wrap around the baby's head, smoothing around the shape and forming a point at the top. Trim away any excess paste at the back and smooth the join closed.

18 Using the green trimmings, roll the stalks and curls to decorate the cake board. Brush a little pink dust colour onto the baby's lips and over the cheeks to give a slight blush.

Extra/alternative requirements for each pea baby:

Edibles

2 x 7cm dome-shaped cakes

A little cake filling (see recipes on pages 12 to 13)

Sugarpaste (rolled fondant):

65g (2¼oz) green (for the body and hat)

Modelling paste:

5g (just under ¼oz) brown/black/pale yellow (for the hair)

55g (2oz) brown/soft beige (for the head and arms)

1 To make a small, ball-shaped cake, sandwich two 7cm (2¾") dome-shaped cakes together using a little cake filling and then spread some filling over the surface so the sugarpaste will stick.

2 Use 60g (2oz) of green sugarpaste to cover each ball completely, smoothing

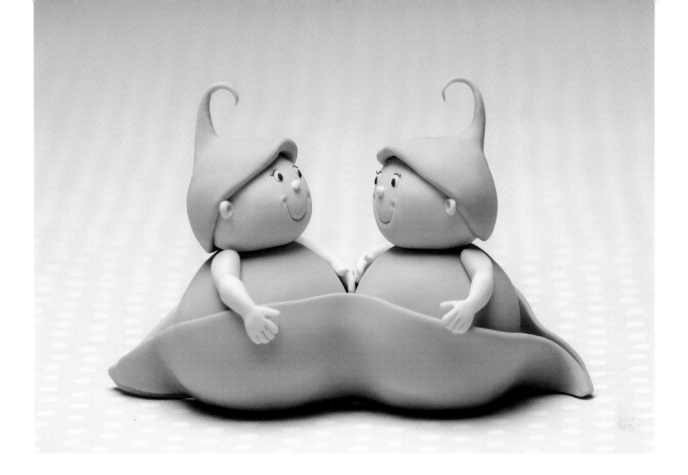

down and around the shape. Roll gently in your hands and then smooth the surface with a small pad of sugarpaste by rubbing gently in a circular motion.

3 Use 45g (1½oz) of soft beige or brown modelling paste for each head and roll into an oval shape. Push a small circle cutter into the bottom to mark the smile, pushing up into the paste and

indenting a semicircle only. Dimple the corners by pushing into the paste with the end of a paintbrush. Roll a tiny, oval-shaped nose and attach with edible glue.

4 Indent two small oval-shaped eye sockets using the small end of a bone or ball tool. Stick two white oval-shapes of modelling paste into the centre for eyes and then two smaller black oval-shapes for the pupils. For the eyelashes, roll minute black pieces of modelling paste between your thumb and index finger, rubbing gently back and forth to make them very fine. Stick each eyelash in place across the top edge of the eyes and curl them up at the corner. Brush a little pink dust colour over each cheek.

5 To make a small hat, roll the paste into a ball, indent the bottom then pinch and smooth around the edge to widen the brim. Pinch at the top to make a point.

6 For the hair, stick on small, flattened pieces of modelling paste in your chosen colour and mark lines on the surface using the end of a paintbrush. For curly hair, break open an unkneaded pack of sugarpaste and slice pieces off the textured surface. Stick pieces around the head. Push in with the end of a paintbrush to disguise the joins. Add a tiny textured ball for the topknot.

7 Split 10g (¼oz) of soft beige modelling paste in half for each pair of arms and then model as for the main cake.

Two Peas in a Pod

Cover two small ball-shaped cakes and stick them together. For the pod, make two opposite sides as before and using 35g (1¼oz) of green modelling paste for each side.

toy box

There's something so pretty about a baby's first toy box stuffed full of their very first soft animals and pre-school toys. I decorated the toy box with images of farmyard animals, but if you're short of time then a large heart or star or even the baby's name spelt with alphabet cutters would look great.

Edibles

2 x 15cm (6") square cakes, each 6cm (2½") depth (see recipes on pages 6 to 9)

400g (14oz) cake filling/crumb coat (see recipes on pages 12 to 13)

Sugarpaste (rolled fondant):

625g (1lb 6oz) lemon

400g (14oz) pale lemon

125g (4½oz) peach

Modelling paste:

tiny piece black

35g (1¼oz) lemon

450g (1lb) pale lemon

115g (4oz) pale peach

90g (3oz) pale yellow

145g (5oz) peach

tiny piece white

340g (12oz) yellow

Edible glue (see recipe on page 15) (SK)

Equipment

Basic equipment (see pages 16 to 18)

30cm (12") square cake board

15cm (6") square cake card/board

Food-safe plastic dowel

2.5cm, 4cm, 5cm and 9cm (1", 1½", 2" and 3½") circle cutters

Blossom cutter

Piping nozzles (tips): nos. 4, 16 (PME)

2 x paper lolly sticks

A few cocktail sticks

Texture mat or new, plastic pan scourer

Cake Board

1 Knead the pale lemon sugarpaste until soft and pliable. Sprinkle the work surface with icing sugar, rub a little onto the top of the sugarpaste and then roll out, moving the paste around to prevent sticking after each roll, until you have a thickness of 2-3mm (⅛") and the paste is large enough to cover the cake board.

2 Moisten the cake board with a little cooled, boiled water or edible glue and then lift and position the sugarpaste onto the board. Smooth the surface with a cake smoother, trim the excess from around the edge and then set aside to dry.

Cake

3 Trim the crust from each cake and level the tops. Place one cake on top of the other. To make room for the toys and create a ridge on which the lid will be supported, cut a 2.5cm (1") deep wedge from the top, leaving a strip of cake 5cm (2") wide that slopes slightly. Cut layers in each cake and sandwich all the layers together with cake filling. Spread a layer over the surface as a crumb coat and to help the sugarpaste stick. Position the cake on the cake board slightly towards the back and use a dab of cake filling to secure.

Toy Box

4 Cover the top of the cake first using the peach sugarpaste. Trim carefully around the top edge so the sides will sit neatly. Roll out the lemon sugarpaste to a thickness of

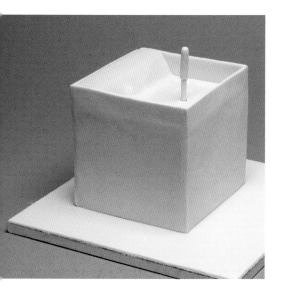

2-4mm (1/8") and cut pieces to cover all sides one at a time. Cover the two sides first then the back and front. Stick the joins closed with edible glue and rub gently to blend the join.

5 Insert the dowelling slightly towards the front and cover the top part with pale lemon sugarpaste trimmings. This will support the lid later and will form the pole for the stacked rings. To hide the joins at the sides of the cake, thinly roll out some pale peach modelling paste and cut strips to edge the cake sides, chamfering the corners.

Lid

6 Cover the cake card with lemon sugarpaste and round off the edge slightly (I covered the back of the board so the silver covering would show underneath the lid). Thickly roll out the pale peach modelling paste and cut chamfered strips to edge the cake card. Use edible glue to secure them in place.

7 To make the chicken's face, thinly roll out some pale peach paste and cut a 9cm (3½") circle. Pick up the circle and stretch the top to lengthen it, making an oval shape.

8 For the beak, cut out a 5cm (2") circle of peach modelling paste and stretch into an oval shape. Cut out two curves at the bottom on either side using a knife and then smooth with your fingertips. Indent the nostrils using the end of a paintbrush. Add small, flattened teardrop shapes for the feathers and add white oval-shaped eyes with smaller, black ovals on top.

9 Using the same technique as for the lid, make all the motifs for the toy box with the horse on the front, the sheep and pig on opposite sides and the cow on the back.

Xylophone

10 Thickly roll out 60g (2oz) of pale lemon modelling paste and cut an oblong for the base measuring 11cm x 3cm (4½"

x 1¼"). To make the bars, cut oblong shapes measuring 4.5cm x 1.5cm (4¾" x ⅝") in pale lemon, lemon, pale yellow, yellow, pale peach and peach. Stick a small yellow ball onto the end of each lolly stick for the beaters and then put everything aside to dry.

Balls

11 Roll two 115g (4oz) balls of modelling paste, one in yellow and the other in pale lemon. Cut both into quarters and then stick alternate sections together, making a striped ball. Decorate with blossom and circle shapes cut from thinly rolled modelling paste. Split the remaining pieces, roll into small balls and stick onto the raised back of the toy box.

Teddy

12 Roll a ball-shaped head with 50g (1¾oz) of pale lemon modelling paste. Roll a 15g (½oz) ball for a muzzle, attach it to the head with edible glue then mark

a line down the centre with the back of a knife. Indent a semicircle smile by pushing in with the smallest circle cutter and dimple the corners using a cocktail stick.

13 Roll a sausage-shaped arm and stick this into the top of the toy box along with the head. Add a peach nose and two eyes as before. Roll two balls for ears, indent the centre of each with the small end of a bone or ball tool and secure in place.

Dog

14 Roll a 35g (1¼oz) ball for his body using pale lemon modelling paste. For his head, roll 50g (1¾oz) of yellow modelling paste into a rounded teardrop shape. To make the muzzle, roll 35g (1¼oz) of pale lemon paste into an oval shape and stick in position against his head, supported on the front of the toy box. Mark the muzzle as before. Roll two small teardrop-shaped ears and add two teardrops on top of his head for hair.

15 Split 15g (½oz) of yellow modelling paste in two for the dog's arms. Roll into sausage shapes first and then roll at the end to round off the paws. Indent the paws with the back of a knife.

Ball Rattle

16 Roll a ball with 20g (¾oz) of pale lemon modelling paste and score a line around the centre using a knife. Make a hole in the bottom ready for the handle using the end of a paintbrush. For the handle, roll a long teardrop of yellow modelling paste and set aside to dry. Decorate the rattle with blossoms and spots as before.

Teether

17 Roll 10g (¼oz) each of yellow, pale lemon and pale peach modelling paste into ball shapes and press down using a cake smoother to flatten. Cut a small hole at the bottom of each disc using

the smallest piping nozzle. Roll two tiny sausages and loop these into the holes, followed by a larger yellow handle. Stick in position at an angle just beyond the support strip.

Building Block

18 Model 30g (1oz) of yellow modelling paste into a cube by pressing with a cake smoother on all sides. Score lines with a knife then decorate with blossom shapes using thinly rolled pale lemon modelling paste.

Hoops

19 Roll 45g (1½oz) of peach modelling paste into a ball and press down to flatten using a cake smoother. Cut a hole in the centre using the smallest circle cutter and smooth around the edge to soften. Stick this in place over the pole. Make two further hoops, one yellow using 35g (1¼oz) of paste and one pale lemon using 20g (¾oz).

20 Roll 15g (½oz) of peach modelling paste into a sausage the width of the toy box and stick this in position along the back. Moisten the top with edible glue and then press the lid in place, pushing into the strip of paste at the back and resting the front on the pole.

Caterpillar

21 Roll 20g (¾oz) of pale lemon paste into a ball shape and press down to flatten using a cake smoother. Use this as the first part of the caterpillar's body. Roll slightly smaller ball shapes graduating in size in pale yellow, pale peach and yellow, finishing with a small ball of pale lemon at the end. Stick these together to form the body of the caterpillar and decorate with blossom shapes and circles.

22 To make the head, roll 30g (1oz) of pale yellow paste into a ball. Use the 4cm (1½") circle cutter to indent the smile by pushing in an upward angle. Dimple the corners using a cocktail stick. Add eyes as before.

23 To make the hat, roll 5g (just under ¼oz) of yellow modelling paste into a ball and press down to flatten, rolling over the surface gently to stretch out the paste. Add a ball to the top and press down to create a dome shape. Add a small blossom.

Rug

24 To create the striped rug, roll out and cut strips of different widths using the remaining modelling paste. Texture the surface by pressing a texture mat or kitchen pan scourer over the paste.

25 Position the first strip across the cake board against the front of the toy box. Add some more to the front and then start layering down the sides, finishing with around two at the back. Assemble the xylophone then add a small, flattened ball of pale lemon to the top of each bar. Place the ball onto the rug, securing with edible glue.

cupcakes

These coordinating cupcakes are very easy to decorate: spread cake filling over the top in a dome shape then cover with a thin layer of sugarpaste in different shades of lemon and yellow to match the cake. Decorate with miniature toys made from modelling paste.

bears

Bears have been a favourite for over a century and although popular toys and characters may take precedence sometimes, the teddy bear will always remain. The soft, muted tones are very pretty here but equally these teddies would look gorgeous in any colourway.

Edibles

2 x 15cm (6"), 2 x 10cm (4") and 2 x 7cm (2¾") bowl-shaped cakes (or one large cupcake/small muffin) (see recipes on pages 6 to 9)

685g (1lb 8oz) cake filling/crumb coat (see recipes on pages 12 to 13)

Icing (powdered) sugar in a sugar shaker

350g (12¼oz) marshmallow rice cereal (see recipe on page 10)

Sugarpaste (rolled fondant):

    5g (just under ¼oz) black

    30g (1oz) brown

    1.3kg (2lb 13¾oz) deep cream

    400g (14oz) pale blue

    200g (7oz) pale brown

    750g (1lb 10½oz) pale cream

Edible glue (see recipe on page 15)

Equipment

Basic equipment (see pages 16 to 18)

30cm (12") square cake board

3 x food-safe plastic dowels

Medium paintbrush (SK)

3cm (1¼") circle cutter

Cake Board

1 Knead the pale blue sugarpaste until soft and pliable. Sprinkle the work surface with icing sugar, rub a little onto the top of the sugarpaste and then roll out, moving the paste around to prevent sticking after each roll, until you have a thickness of 2-3mm (¹⁄₈") and the paste is large enough to cover the cake board.

2 Moisten the cake board with a little cooled, boiled water or edible glue and then lift and position the sugarpaste onto the board. Smooth the surface with a cake smoother, trim the excess from around the edge. Indent two deep lines using a ruler and then mark the wood grain effect with the back of a knife. Set aside to dry.

Bear Heads

3 For the large bear, mould 225g (8oz) of marshmallow and rice cereal mixture together whilst it is still slightly warm and make a 10cm (4") ball following the instructions on page 10. Push a food-safe dowel 5cm (2") deep into the base and then remove. For the medium sized bear use 100g (3½oz) and for the small bear use 25g (just over ¾oz) of the cereal mixture, indent holes as before but make it a little shorter for the small bear. Put aside to set for around 10 minutes.

4 Once each head is set, use small pieces of sugarpaste to fill in any uneven areas and then brush the surface with edible glue. Alternatively, use ganache to create a smooth surface (see Tip on page 54). Roll out 300g (10½oz) of deep

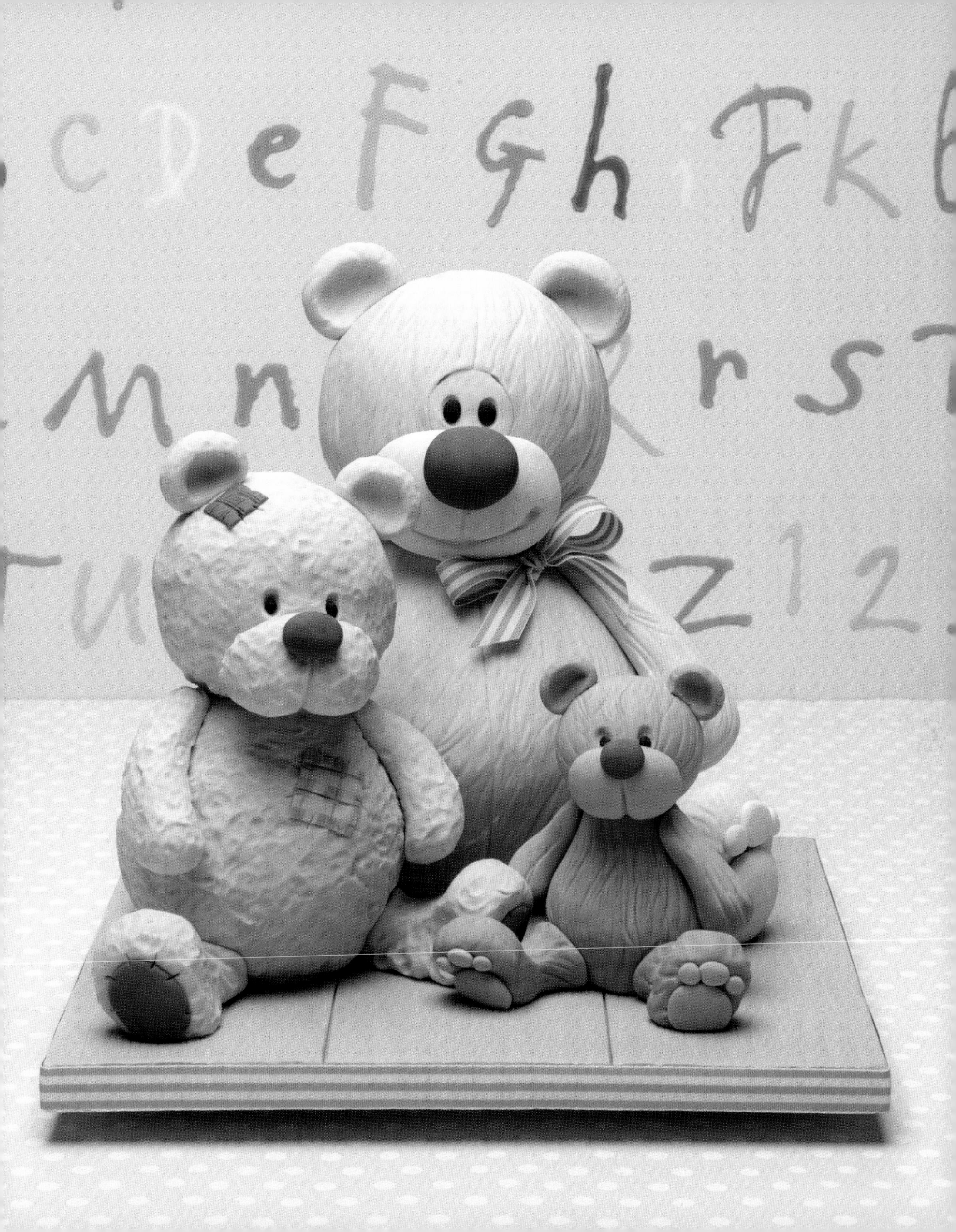

cream sugarpaste and cover the large ball completely, smoothing around the shape and trimming away any excess paste from around the back. Brush the join with a little edible glue and smooth it closed. Smooth the surface with your hands or use a spare piece of sugarpaste rolled into a ball to rub over the surface.

> ## tip
>
> If you would prefer to use cake to make the heads, bake in dome-shaped pans to the diameter required, sandwich together and position on a small cake board. You will need to insert three dowels down through the body that are cut level with the top so the head is well supported.

5 Mark a circle in the centre of the face using the circle cutter and indent two eye sockets using your fingertip. To create the texture of fur, stroke a paintbrush handle

or modelling tool over the surface from the top to the base.

6 Cover the medium sized marshmallow ball with 125g (4½oz) of pale cream sugarpaste and texture the surface by pressing in lightly with your fingertips. Indent eye sockets with the paintbrush handle, using a circular motion to open them up.

7 Cover the small bear's head with a little pale brown sugarpaste then mark lines on the surface and indent eye sockets as before. Set all three heads aside for later.

Bodies

8 Trim the crust from each cake and level the tops. Cut a layer in each cake and then put both halves together to make ball shapes. If preferred, you can use an upside down cupcake or muffin for the smallest bear. Trim around the top of each cake to narrow it slightly: this helps to round off the tummy area. Sandwich the layers together with cake filling and then spread a layer

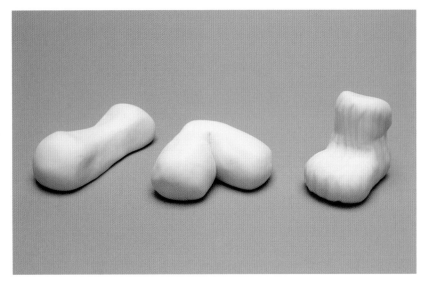

over the surface of each cake to seal in the crumbs and help the sugarpaste stick.

9 To cover the large bear's body, roll out 450g (1lb) of deep cream sugarpaste and cover the cake completely, smoothing around the shape, stretching out any pleats and smoothing downwards. Trim off the excess paste from around the base or tuck it underneath the cake to round off the bottom. Mark the texture by stroking the paintbrush handle over the surface, starting from the bottom and stroking in an upwards motion. Position this cake on the cake board so the body is central but level with the back.

10 Cover the medium sized teddy's body in the same way using 260g (9oz) of pale cream sugarpaste. Indent the fur texture by pressing in with your fingertips as before.

11 Cover the smallest bear in the same way using pale brown sugarpaste then mark the fur effect with the paintbrush handle. Position each on the cake board, leaving enough space for the bear's legs, and secure with a little edible glue.

Legs and Feet

12 To make the large bear's legs, split 300g (10½oz) of deep cream sugarpaste in half and roll into fat sausage shapes. Bending one end of each leg round to form the foot then squeeze gently on either side to lengthen and narrow each foot. Mark lines as before. Cut the top off each leg at an angle and then stick in position. Add pale cream circles of sugarpaste on each foot to make the pads.

13 Make the medium bear and small bear's legs as before and texture in the same way as their bodies; you will need 145g (5oz) of sugarpaste for the medium bear and 75g (2½oz) for the small bear.

14 Glue a brown oval-shaped pad onto the bottom of each foot for the medium bear, then mark stitching with the tip of a knife. Roll out a little brown paste and cut a square for the brown patch on his head, marking the pattern and stitching with a knife. Make pads for the small bear from pale brown sugarpaste and secure to the feet with edible glue.

Arms

15 Split 200g (7oz) of deep cream sugarpaste in half to make the large bear's arms. First moisten either side of the body with edible glue and leave to become sticky. Roll the sugarpaste into sausage shapes, rounding off one end of each and then press into position. Texture as before.

16 Make the arms for the remaining bears using 75g (2½oz) of pale cream for the medium bear and 20g (¾oz) of pale brown for the small bear. Texture to match the body of each bear.

Faces

17 Moisten the bottom half of the large bear's face with edible glue ready for his muzzle and leave for a few moments for the surface to become sticky. Roll 75g (2½oz) of pale cream sugarpaste into an oval shape and press down on the work surface to flatten slightly. Press in position against the glue, holding for a few moments until secure.

18 Using the paintbrush handle, mark a semicircle smile and then use the bristles of the paintbrush to stroke back and forth, opening up the mouth at the bottom and in the two corners. Mark a line from the centre of the mouth upwards. Pinch the paste gently at the bottom to shape a chin.

19 Make the muzzles for the two remaining bears using 45g (1½oz) for the medium bear and 15g (½oz) for the small bear. Stick in position then mark a central line with the paintbrush handle and stroke the paste upwards.

20 Make all the noses using brown sugarpaste and all the oval-shaped eyes in black. Stick the noses and eyes in position with edible glue.

Ears

21 Split the remaining deep cream sugarpaste in half and roll into ball shapes for the large bear's ears. Press down into the centre of each to create a dip and then cut the bottom of each one straight. Stick in position and texture as before. Make the remaining bears' ears using pale cream for the medium bear and pale brown for the small bear.

Patch

22 To make the patch on the medium bear's chest, roll out a small piece of pale cream sugarpaste as thinly as possible using a good sprinkling of icing sugar. Cut small strips for the stripes and set aside. Thinly roll out a little pale brown sugarpaste and then stick the strips in a criss-cross pattern on top with a little edible glue. Press down to ensure they will not move and to check there is no excess glue and then roll over the paste gently with a rolling pin to inlay the pattern. Cut out a small square and then mark lines with a knife. Stick in position on the medium bear's body and mark stitching around the outside edge with a knife.

mini bears

These are made in exactly the same way as the small bear in the main project, just change the colour and texture and their poses. A group of them together in different positions looks fantastic.

Extra/alternative requirements for each cake:

Edibles

2 x 7cm (2¾") bowl-shaped cakes (or one large cupcake/small muffin) for each body

25g (just over ¾oz) marshmallow rice cereal (see recipe on page 10)

Sugarpaste (rolled fondant):

   tiny piece black

   220g (8oz) in your chosen shade of brown

   5g (just under ¼oz) dark golden brown

Equipment

Paper lolly sticks (optional)

1 Make the bears in the same way as described for the main cake in your chosen shade of brown. You will need 30g (1oz) of sugarpaste to cover the head, 75g (2½oz) for the body, 20g (¾oz) for both arms, 75g (2½oz) for both legs, 15g (½oz) for the muzzle and 5g (just under ¼oz) for the ears. If the arms or legs are in a raised position, use paper lolly sticks for extra support where required.

2 Add the nose and feet pads in dark brown and finish with tiny black eyes.

bear faces

Shown here with alternative colours you can see exactly how different they can all look – even the main cake can include bears that are all pink or all blue or any other colour in pretty, subtle shades.

Extra/alternative requirements for each cake:

Edibles

7cm (2¾") dome-shaped cake (baked in an ovenproof silicone bowl or mould)

A little cake filling (see recipes on pages 12 to 13)

Sugarpaste:

    tiny amount black

    45g (1½oz) in your choice of colours

Equipment

Small, round cake cards or circles of greaseproof paper

tip

To make the cakes for the mini bear heads you could also use stainless steel sundae dishes or small ovenproof glass bowls available from kitchenware specialists or the homeware department in most supermarkets.

1 Place each cake on the same sized thin cake card or use a disc of greaseproof paper to protect the uncovered cake/surface underneath. Cover the surface with a thin layer of cake filling then roll out 35g (1¼oz) of sugarpaste to cover the cake and smooth it around the shape. Use a knife to trim away the excess paste or tuck it underneath for a more rounded look.

2 Use 35g (1¼oz) of sugarpaste for the muzzle and 10g (¼oz) for each ear and make them in the same way as for the large bears. Attach in place with edible glue. Mark eye sockets and a mouth and texture as before. Finally, add two tiny ovals of black paste for the eyes.

fairytale castles

Two castles, one fit for your handsome little prince or your pretty princess, both in soft baby shades of either pink or blue. I included another timeless favourite by adding a teddy bear here and there, with two soldier bears guarding the entrance.

blue castle

Edibles

15cm (6") square and 10cm (4") round cakes, each (3") depth (see recipes on pages 6 to 9)

450g (1lb) cake filling/crumb coat (see recipes on pages 12 to 13)

Sugarpaste (rolled fondant):

  800g (1lb 12oz) blue

  210g (7½oz) pale blue

Modelling paste:

  tiny piece black (optional)

  20g (¾oz) blue

  700g (1lb 8¾oz) pale blue

  10g (¼oz) soft beige

  5g (just under ¼oz) white

Dust food colours: blue, pink (SK)

Paste or liquid food colour: black (SK)

Edible glue (see recipe on page 15) (SK)

Sugar stick or small length of raw, dried spaghetti (see page 15)

Equipment

Basic equipment (see pages 16 to 18)

30cm (12") cake board, round for pink castle or square for blue castle

8cm (3") round cake card

3 x food-safe plastic dowels

Fine and medium paintbrushes (SK)

Small piece of card

Templates (see page 111)

1.5cm (⅝") square cutter

A few cocktail sticks

Piping nozzles (tips): nos. 1, 2, 17 (PME)

Cake Board

1 Knead 400g (14oz) of pale blue sugarpaste for the blue castle until soft and pliable. Sprinkle the work surface with icing sugar, rub a little onto the top of the sugarpaste and then roll out, moving the paste around to prevent sticking after each roll, until you have a thickness of 2-3mm (⅛") and the paste is large enough to cover the cake board.

2 Moisten the cake board with a little cooled, boiled water or edible glue and then lift and position the sugarpaste onto the board. Smooth the surface with a cake smoother, trim the excess from around the edge and then set aside to dry.

Cakes

3 Trim the crust from both cakes and level the tops. Cut layers in the cakes and sandwich back together with cake filling. Spread a thin layer of filling over the surface of each cake as a crumb coat to seal the cake and help the sugarpaste stick. Position the large cake centrally on the covered cake board and the smaller cake on the cake card.

4 Cover the sides separately to achieve a sharp top edge so the battlements sit straight. Roll out 75g (2½oz) of blue sugarpaste and cut an oblong to cover the

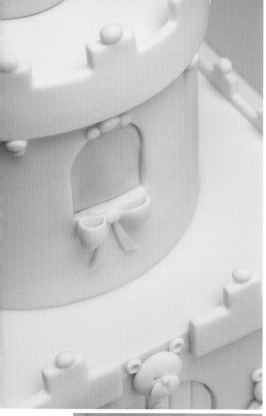

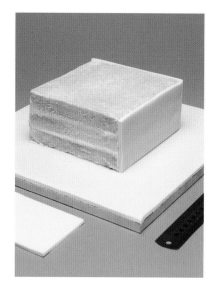

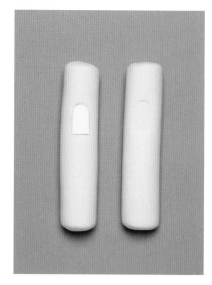

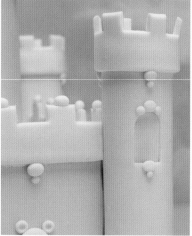

front of the cake, using a ruler to measure it accurately. Repeat for the remaining three sides. Roll out the remaining blue sugarpaste and cut a piece to cover the top, ensuring the join is as neat as possible.

tip

If you have a very stretchy sugarpaste that can be rolled quite thin without tearing you can cover the large cake in one piece and then use a cake smoother to create a sharp top edge.

5 The weight of the top tier may not be supported by the bottom tier, so it is a good idea to dowel the bottom tier. Push the three dowels down into the centre of the cake within an 8cm (3") diameter. Mark each dowel level with the top of the sugarpaste and then remove. Cut the dowels to the same size, level with the lowest mark (to ensure there are no gaps

between the tiers). Cover the smaller cake following instructions for covering the base of the pink castle using 210g (7½oz) of pale blue sugarpaste (see page 78). Place the cake onto a cake card of the same size then position on top of the bottom tier, securing with a little edible glue.

6 Using the door and large window templates, cut out the doorframe and window at the front of the top tier and remove the sugarpaste. Thinly roll out 10g (¼oz) of pale blue paste and cut out the door shape. Mark lines using the ruler and then secure in position with edible glue. Thinly roll out the same paste and fill the window.

Turrets

7 The blue castle has four turrets, one at each corner to hide the joins. Use 100g (3½oz) of light blue modelling paste for each one. Roll the paste into a sausage shape 13cm (5") in length and cut each end straight. Use 75g (2½oz) of paste to make the top turret, this time measuring

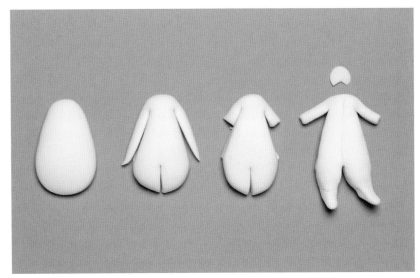

6cm (2¼") in height. Indent all the windows by pressing the small window template cut from a piece of card into the surface. Lay the taller turrets down flat to dry and stick the top turret in position.

Battlements

8 To make the battlements, cut 2.5cm (1") strips from thinly rolled-out modelling paste and cut out squares from along the top using the small square cutter. Attach the battlements starting at the top of the cake, then use them to decorate around the top edge of the top turret. Stick the turrets in position once dry then make battlements for the bottom tier.

9 Make the door handle and secure in place with edible glue. For the bow, roll two large pea-sized pieces of blue modelling paste into tapered sausage shapes and press down to flatten. Make each one into a loop and stick with edible glue. Roll out and cut two ribbons, stick in position with the loops and add a small, flattened ball in the centre for the knot.

Teddy Bears

10 The bears decorating each castle are made with pale blue or pale pink modelling paste. Roll two teardrop shapes for the soldiers' bodies first, flatten and stick in position on either side of the door. To make the legs, use a pea-sized piece for each, roll into small sausage shapes and bend one end round for the foot. Stick small sausages for arms on either side. Roll a ball for each head, a smaller ball for each muzzle and press down to flatten before sticking in position. Mark each muzzle with a knife. Indent eyes using a cocktail stick.

Add two tiny ears on each bear and indent with the end of a paintbrush. Make bows as before for their necks.

11 Make a bear's head for above the door and one to go on the door, adding a tiny loop of modelling paste underneath for the door knocker.

12 The baby's toy bear at the front of the cake is made using blue or pale pink modelling paste. Model as before but indent a smile using a no. 17 piping nozzle pushed in at an upwards angle and dimple the corners with a cocktail stick. Add two tiny black eyes cut from a no. 1 nozzle. Make small holes for the legs to slot in and support until dry.

Baby's Pyjamas

13 To make the baby's all-in-one, roll 20g (¾oz) of pale blue modelling paste into a rounded teardrop shape and press down to flatten slightly. Make a cut on either side at the narrow end to separate the sleeves and then cut at the bottom to

separate the legs. Stroke gently to remove the ridges and round off both the sleeves and legs. Pinch near the tip of each leg to make the feet. Cut the sleeves straight and indent a small hole in each one ready for the hands later.

14 Mark down the centre with a knife then make tiny holes for poppers using a cocktail stick. To make the collar, roll a pea-sized ball of pale blue modelling paste and press down to flatten. Cut out a small section from one side and then stick the collar in place.

Hands

15 Roll two small teardrop shapes using a pea-sized amount of soft beige modelling paste for each hand and press down to flatten slightly. Cut the thumbs on opposite sides and then make three cuts along the top to separate the fingers. Gently squeeze the fingers together, stroking them gently to lengthen slightly and then push the thumbs down towards each palm to shape the hands into a natural pose. Stick each hand in place using a little edible glue.

Head

16 Push a sugar stick or length of raw spaghetti down into the body, leaving around 2cm (¾") protruding ready to support the head. Put aside a tiny piece of soft beige modelling paste for the nose and ears later and then roll the remainder into a ball. Pinch around the cheek area to make it fuller on one side and repeat on the opposite side. Stroke down from the centre to flatten the mouth area and pinch on either side to form a chin at the bottom. Indent two eye sockets using the end of a paintbrush.

17 Indent the smile by pushing a no. 17 piping nozzle in at an upward angle to create a semicircle and dimple each corner using a cocktail stick. Add a tiny ball for the nose and indent nostrils with a cocktail stick. Roll two minute balls of white for the eyes and add black pupils cut from black paste with the no. 2 piping nozzle or painted using black food colouring and a fine paintbrush. Paint the eyelashes. Roll two tiny balls for ears, indent the centre of each with the end of a

paintbrush and then stick in position using a little edible glue. Dust the cheeks with a little pink dust colour.

Crown

18 Add a small, flattened ball to the top of the baby's head as the base of the crown. Stick flattened pieces of white paste over the head then use a damp paintbrush to texture the surface. Add a second flattened ball to the crown, slightly smaller than before and make another the same size but flattened more so it is wider and thinner. Roll out some more paste, cut four long triangles measuring 1cm (³/₈") and stick them evenly around the top of the crown. Add a tiny ball on the top of each point.

Finishing Touches

19 Use blue modelling paste to make a small bear face to decorate the nightwear. Dust around the base of the cake and at the windows using blue dust colour.

pink castle

The design can be adapted easily to make a pink castle for a little princess. You will need to substitute the blue sugarpaste and modelling paste for pink and make a few alterations to the design, as described overleaf.

Edibles

18cm (7") and 10cm (4") round cakes, each (3") depth (see recipes on pages 6 to 9)

450g (1lb) cake filling/crumb coat (see recipes on pages 12 to 13)

Sugarpaste (rolled fondant):

   210g (7½oz) pale pink

   750g (1lb 10½oz) pink

Modelling paste:

   tiny piece black (optional)

   600g (1lb 5¼oz) pale pink

   20g (¾oz) pink

   10g (¼oz) soft beige

   5g (just under ¼oz) white

Dust food colour: pink (SK)

Paste or liquid food colour: black (SK)

Edible glue (see recipe on page 15) (SK)

Sugar stick or small length of raw, dried spaghetti (see page 15)

Equipment

See equipment for blue castle but substitute the 30cm (12") square cake board for a round one.

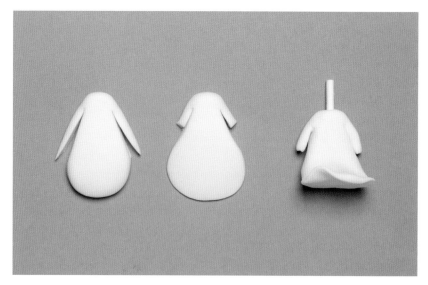

1 To cover the cake board, roll out 315g (11oz) of pale pink sugarpaste and cover the board in the usual way.

2 To cover the large cake, roll out 300g (10½oz) of pink sugarpaste and cut a strip to cover the sides of the largest cake. Dust with icing sugar and then roll up carefully. Position the rolled up sugarpaste against the cake sides, lined up where one of the turrets will be positioned so the join will be hidden, and unroll the paste around the cake. Trim away the excess from the join and close by adding a little edible glue and smoothing gently. Roll out the remaining pink sugarpaste and cover the top of the cake. Smooth with a cake smoother and then trim around the top edge, keeping it as neat as possible so the battlements sit straight.

3 Dowel the bottom tier as before then cover the top tier, place on a cake card and position on top of the large cake.

4 Make the windows and doors as described for the blue castle. When you are making the turrets the pink castle has two, one on either side of the door. Follow the same instructions as for the blue castle but using light pink modelling paste. Secure the turrets in place then add battlements around the tops of the cakes. Add a door handle as before.

5 For the pointed roofs, split 120g (4¼oz) of pale pink modelling paste into three pieces, one slightly larger than the other two. Roll the larger piece into a teardrop shape and press down on the full end to flatten it. Stroke the sides and pinch gently to widen the base and then stick in position on the top turret. Make the two smaller roofs for the turrets on either side of the door in the same way and secure in place.

6 Decorate the battlements and around the windows of the pink castle with small balls of modelling paste. Add a bow as before.

7 Follow the instructions to make the teddies for either side of the door and make bear heads for above the door and the door knocker. Add bear heads and bows to the top of each roof on the pink castle. Model a toy bear for the little girl as before.

8 Make a nightgown for the baby instead of pyjamas. Roll a 15g (½oz) teardrop of pale pink modelling paste and press down to flatten slightly. Make a cut on each side for the sleeves and smooth gently to round off. Cut off any excess paste at the bottom and indent a small hole ready for the hands later. Smooth down at the bottom to thin and frill the paste slightly. Bend the nightgown halfway into a sitting position.

9 Make the head, face and hands as before. Add a crown to the baby's head and a bear's head to the nightgown.

10 Dust around the base of the cake and at the windows using pink dust colour.

mini castle cakes

These can be cut from any size cake depending on how many you need to make. I have used 5cm (2") cakes which can be cut from a large cake, measuring carefully for the squares or using a circle cutter to cut the rounds. Alternatively you can bake batches of round or square mini cakes using mini cake pans (available from sugarcraft suppliers, see page 112).

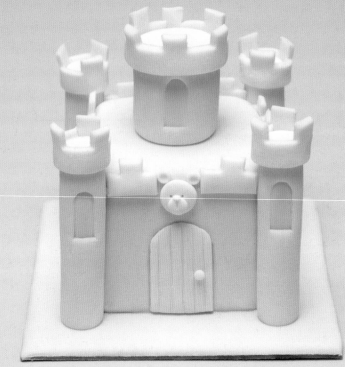

Extra/alternative requirements for each castle:

Edibles

5cm (2") round or square mini cake, 4cm (1½") depth

A little cake filling (see recipes on pages 12 to 13)

Sugarpaste (rolled fondant):
    200g (7oz) pale blue or 175g (6oz) pale pink

Equipment

10cm (4") round or square cake card

1cm (³/₈") square cutter

Templates*

*Cut the templates slightly smaller than for the main cake: the door should measure 2cm x 3cm (¾" x 1¼") and the windows 0.5cm x 1.5cm (¼" x ½"). Curve both the door and windows slightly at the top.

1 Roll out some pale blue or pink sugarpaste thinly and cover the cake card. Trim neatly around the edge.

2 Layer and fill the mini cake; this will increase the depth to around 4.5cm-5cm (1¾"-2"). To cover, thinly roll out the remaining sugarpaste and cover over the shape completely, smoothing down and around the sides. Use a cake smoother to polish the surface and remove any imperfections. Trim away the excess paste from around the base; for the round cakes

you can use a circle cutter slightly larger than the cake. Place the cake in the centre of the covered cake card.

3 Roll a small cylinder of paste and stick this to the top of the castle with edible glue.

4 Roll out the remaining sugarpaste and make the battlements in the same way as for the main cake using a 1cm (³/₈") square cutter. Add pointed roofs on the pink castle then add the door, windows and teddy detail as for the main cake.

cupcake crowns

The mini castles are very appealing but they are also quite time consuming if you have multiple servings. An alternative idea is to fill up the party table and increase servings with these extremely simple crown cupcakes. Use a standard size cupcake and spread cake filling over the top in a dome shape. Cover with a thin layer of sugarpaste cut from a 7cm (2¾") circle cutter (or a size to fit your cupcakes).

Make the crowns in advance from 20g (¾oz) of modelling paste (see main cake for instructions) then place on top of the freshly covered cupcake. If you have many to make, you can use a tiny cutter to make the circles on the points of the crown.

baby blocks

This design was inspired by watching a special one-year-old named Hannah repeatedly stack bricks in her trolley. She piled up other toys also, taking great delight in emptying her toy box, one by one, much to the amusement of everyone, until it became time to tidy up, of course.

Edibles

20cm (8") square cake and 2 x 10cm (4") square cakes, each 5cm (2") depth (see recipes on pages 6 to 9)

685g (1lb 8oz) cake filling/crumb coat (see recipes on pages 12 to 13)

Sugarpaste (rolled fondant):

   175g (6oz) blue

   315g (11oz) lilac

   1.14kg (2lb 8oz) white

Modelling paste:

   tiny piece black

   200g (7oz) blue

   20g (¾oz) green

   20g (¾oz) lemon

   20g (¾oz) lilac

   20g (¾oz) pink

   310g (10¾oz) white

Edible glue (see recipe on page 15) (SK)

Equipment

Basic equipment (see pages 16 to 18)

30cm (12") square cake board

2 x 8cm (3") square cake cards

6 x food-safe plastic dowels

Fine and medium paintbrushes (SK)

Large alphabet cutters

3 x paper lolly sticks

Miniature star cutter

Piping nozzles (tips): nos. 3, 4, 16, 18 (PME)

Cake Board

1 Knead 400g (14oz) of white sugarpaste until soft and pliable. Sprinkle the work surface with icing sugar, rub a little onto the top of the sugarpaste and then roll out, moving the paste around to prevent sticking after each roll, until you have a thickness of 2-3mm (¹/₈") and the paste is large enough to cover the cake board.

2 Moisten the cake board with a little cooled, boiled water or edible glue and then lift and position the sugarpaste onto the board. Smooth the surface with a cake smoother, trim the excess from around the edge and then set aside to dry.

Cake

3 Trim the crust from each cake and level the tops. To make the oblong-shaped walker, cut an 8cm (3") strip from the larger square cake and set this aside for later. Cut layers in the remaining piece and sandwich back together with cake filling. Spread a layer of filling over the surface of the cake as a crumb coat to seal the cake and help the sugarpaste stick then position the cake at an angle on the covered cake board.

4 Take the remaining strip of cake, cut a 5cm (2") piece from one end and set aside. Cut the other piece in half and stack one piece on top of the other, trimming a little off the height to make into a perfect cube measuring 8cm (3"). Trim the 5cm (2") piece into a perfect cube. Cut layers in each, sandwich with only a little filling so as not to raise the height too much

or cause any bulges in the covering and crumb coat as before. Position the 8cm (3") cube onto one of the cake cards, securing with a dab of cake filling.

5 To make the large cube, sandwich the two 10cm (4") square cakes together checking that they make a perfect cube and then spread a crumb coat as before. Position the cake on the remaining cake card.

Trolley

6 Roll out 175g (6oz) of white sugarpaste, cover the top of the trolley and trim a neat edge. Use a cake smoother to create a dimple-free surface. Thickly roll out the blue sugarpaste and cut pieces to fit the opposite ends exactly, making them 1cm-2cm ($^3/_8$"-$^3/_4$") taller than the height of the cake. Trim the top corners to round off slightly.

7 Using the lilac sugarpaste, repeat to cover the opposite sides, cutting each slightly higher than the ends and rounding

off the top edges by smoothing with your fingertips. Carefully press in position using a cake smoother (you may need to rework the crumb coat if it has set so the sides will stick).

Wheels

8 Split 160g (5½oz) of blue modelling paste into quarters and roll into ball shapes. Press down on each with a cake smoother and then indent the centre of each one by stroking with your fingertips. Stick a small, flattened ball of lilac onto the centre of each and then set the wheels aside to dry.

Cubes

9 Roll out some white sugarpaste and cover all the sides of the cubes separately to create a sharp, neat edge. Do not be concerned about the joins as these will be covered by the pastel strips. To cover each side, roll out the sugarpaste a little at a time, place a cube down onto it and

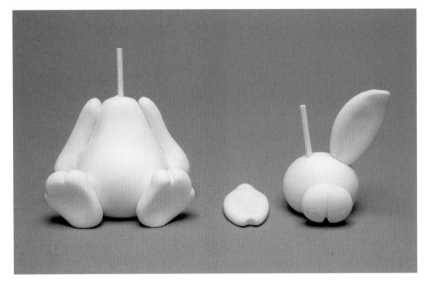

cut around the shape. Repeat for all sides, picking up the cubes using cake smoothers on the covered sides so as not to damage the surface. Stick all the joins closed with a little edible glue. Only cover the base of the smallest cube as the other cubes are placed on cake cards.

10 Push three dowels down into the centre of the trolley cake, keeping them evenly spaced and no more than 8cm (3") apart. Make a mark level with the top and then remove. Place together on the work surface and cut to the lowest mark

if they measure differently; this ensures subsequent tiers will sit straight even if the cake isn't level. Push the dowels back into the cake and then position the large cube on top, securing with a little edible glue. Dowel the large cube ready to support the middle cube but keep it separate for now.

11 To edge the cubes with coloured strips, thinly roll out some modelling paste and cut 1cm ($^3/_8$") deep for the bottom and middle cube and 0.5cm ($^1/_8$") deep for the smallest cube. Stick in place and chamfer each corner to fit neatly. Assemble the cubes on the cake board, securing with a little edible glue around the edges. Cut out the letters to spell 'baby'. Use the piping nozzle and star cutter to cut out all the circles and stars to decorate the cubes. Stick the wheels in position on the walker.

Rabbit

12 To make the body of the rabbit, roll 125g (4½oz) of white modelling paste into a large teardrop shape. Stick this against the trolley and smooth a rounded tummy.

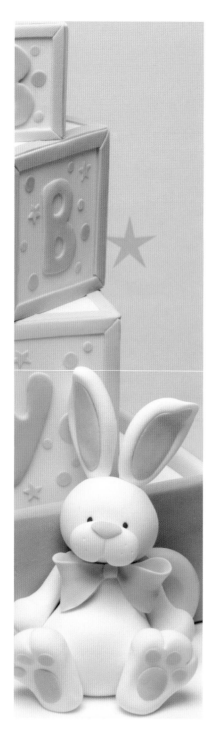

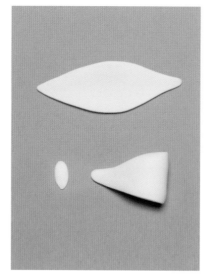

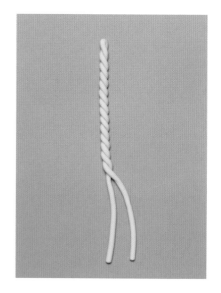

Split 30g (1oz) of white modelling paste in half and roll into sausage shapes for the arms. Round off the end of each for paws and indent twice using the back of a knife.

13 To make the feet, split 45g (1½oz) of white modelling paste in half and roll into rounded teardrop shapes. Press down on each one to flatten slightly and then push the back of a knife into the wide end twice to indent toes. Stick in position then add small, flattened balls of pink for the foot pads.

14 Roll 75g (2½oz) of white modelling paste into an oval shape for the head and stick in position, using a lolly stick to help hold it in place. Add a flattened ball for the muzzle and mark down the centre with the back of a knife. Push the remaining two lolly sticks into the head ready to hold the ears in position.

15 To make the rabbit's ears, split the remaining white paste in two and roll into long teardrop shapes. Indent the centre of

each with your fingertip gently so as not to flatten them too much. Fill the indent with a long, flattened teardrop of pink paste. Moisten the lolly sticks with glue and then gently push each ear down over the lolly stick, securing at the bottom. Add a pink nose and two tiny black eyes.

Finishing Touches

16 Roll a small ball of the lilac trimmings and press down to flatten. Stick in position at the front of the trolley and indent a hole in the centre using the end of a paintbrush. Roll a long sausage of blue modelling paste and twist together to make the rope.

17 To make the bow, reserve a small ball then split the remaining blue paste in half and roll into tapering sausage shapes. Press down to flatten and loop over. Stick in position on the rabbit with a small ball in the centre for the tie.

mini cake cubes

These are 5cm (2") cubes which I find are the perfect size, not too big but just enough for a treat.

Extra/alternative requirements for each cube:

Edibles

5cm (2") cube of cake

A little cake filling or jam (see recipes on pages 12 to 13)

Sugarpaste (rolled fondant):
   75g (2½oz) white sugarpaste

Modelling paste:
   10g (¼oz) in a colour of your choice

Equipment

5cm (2") square of parchment/ greaseproof paper

1 If you would like to layer the cake in the usual way using cake filling, adjust the height of the cake to ensure the overall measurement doesn't change. I prefer to keep them as they are and inject the centre with cake filling, or even just plain jam. This is relatively easy and much quicker if you have lots to do: fill a piping bag and cut a small hole in the tip, then insert into the cake, give a gentle squeeze and remove.

2 To protect the bottom of each cube, cut a square of parchment/greaseproof paper and stick it to the cake with a little cake filling.

3 Roll out some sugarpaste to cover the cake. To do this quickly it can be covered over the top and down the sides in one, rather than each side separately as on the main cake. This works here because the cubes are so much smaller so the sugarpaste doesn't tear so easily and can be rolled thinner, making it easier to create a sharper edge. However, if you only have a few to do you may find you prefer to cover them separately to ensure a perfectly sharp edge every time.

4 Decorate the cube with numbers or letters and add little circles as for the main cake.

cute Kittens

The original design was for a special little girl named Hannah for her first birthday. The design proved so popular I thought it would be nice to include a similar design here. At the party I wished I'd made a few extra kittens positioned around the party table, seemingly attempting to steal the party food.

Edibles

25cm (10") square cake (see recipes on pages 6 to 9)

6 x 7cm (2¾") dome-shaped cakes (see recipes on pages 6 to 9)

450g (1lb) cake filling/crumb coat (see recipes on pages 12 to 13)

160g (5½oz) marshmallow rice cereal (see recipe on page 10)

Sugarpaste:

370g (13oz) blue

900g (2lb) pale blue

15g (½oz) pale pink

975g (2lb 2½oz) white

Edible glue (see recipe on page 15) (SK)

Equipment

Basic equipment (see pages 16 to 18)

35cm (14") square cake board

10cm (4") round cake card/thin board

Fine and medium paintbrushes (SK)

6 x food-safe dowels

18 white food-safe flower stamens or thick cotton thread

A few cocktail sticks

Cushion Cake

1 Trim the crust from the cake, keeping a slightly rounded top. Trim along the top edge to halfway all the way around so it slopes down gently. Turn the cake over and repeat to create the cushion shape.

2 Cut layers in the cake and sandwich back together with cake filling, assembling the cake on the cake board at a slight angle. Spread a layer of filling over the surface of the cake to help the sugarpaste stick.

3 Knead the pale blue sugarpaste until soft and pliable. Using a sprinkling of

icing sugar to prevent sticking, roll out the sugarpaste to a thickness of 2-3mm (1/8"), moving it around after each roll until it is large enough to cover the cake completely. Place the rolling pin on the centre of the rolled out paste, carefully fold the paste over the rolling pin, then lift the paste and position it over the cake, rolling the paste into place. Smooth around the shape with your hands, tucking the excess paste underneath, and trim neatly around the base.

4 Using a paintbrush handle or pointed modelling tool, indent a small channel around the cake ready for the piping. Use

the same paintbrush/tool to indent small pleats around the edges then mark a cross on the top to divide the cake into four.

5 Thinly roll out 60g (2oz) of the slightly darker blue sugarpaste and cut ten stripes to decorate the cushion. Stick them in place on opposite corners of the cushion and smooth the cut edge of each stripe with your fingertip. Moisten along the channel with edible glue then roll a very long, thin sausage for the piping and stick it in place.

6 For the fabric effect on the cake board, first moisten the board with a little edible glue. Thinly roll out white sugarpaste a little at a time and drape and fold this over the cake board. Trim away any excess paste from around the edge.

7 The weight of the kittens could sink down into the centre of the cake so to prevent this from happening, the cushion cake needs to be dowelled. Push three dowels down through the centre of the cake, keeping them no more than 8cm (3") apart. Mark each one level with the

sugarpaste and then remove. Cut to the lowest mark if all measure differently (so the kittens sit level) and then re-insert into the cake. Place the small cake card centrally on top and secure with edible glue.

Kittens

8 It is advisable to use marshmallow rice cereal balls to make the kittens' heads to keep them light: as they are positioned one on top of the other, too much weight bearing down on their bodies could cause them to collapse, even with the dowelling support. Split the warm marshmallow cereal mixture into three and roll into ball shapes, each around 7cm (2¾") in diameter, then

flatten one side slightly for the face. Push a dowel into the bottom of the first two and into the back of the head for the third and leave it there until after the heads are covered. Put aside to set.

9 For the bodies, sandwich the small dome-shaped cakes together in pairs to make three ball-shaped cakes and spread cake filling over the surface to help the sugarpaste stick. Using 90g (3oz) of sugarpaste for each kitten (two white and one blue), roll out the paste and cover the cake completely, smoothing around the shape and pinching the join closed. Pinch the excess sugarpaste up to form the neck and cut straight at the top. Mark a fur effect using a pointed modelling tool or a paintbrush handle.

tip

You can make the kittens totally in cake but I would recommend using chocolate ganache as the crumb coat. Leave the cakes to firm in the refrigerator before decorating so they will support each other well. If you would like to keep the kittens as a memento of the day they can be made totally in marshmallow rice cereal mixture as it lasts much longer than cake.

10 Ensure the surface of each marshmallow rice cereal ball is smooth and if not, add small pieces of sugarpaste into the crevices to even the surface. Brush with edible glue and then use 75g (2½oz) of sugarpaste to cover each head completely. Smooth around the shape then cut any excess paste away at the back and smooth the join closed. Using the paintbrush handle or modelling tool, stroke the surface of each to indent a fur effect. Remove the dowel, ensuring that there is still a hole in the sugarpaste.

11 For the blue kitten's head, thinly roll out 20g (¾oz) of blue sugarpaste and cover the back only, bringing some around the front to frame the face. Texture the paste as before, ensuring the edge of the paste is ragged and fur-like.

12 To make the pointed whiskers, roll teardrop shapes of white and/or blue sugarpaste, press flat and then stick onto the kittens' faces with edible glue. Smooth the whiskers against the surface to remove and blend the join, then texture as before.

13 Build up either side of the face using different sized teardrop shapes and add some around the top of the forehead, blending and texturing as before. If the joins are stubborn, moisten the paintbrush with a little edible glue and brush over the surface; this will dissolve the surface slightly and help blend it. Indent eye sockets using your fingertip just below halfway and stroke around the outside to soften the opening.

14 For the muzzles, split 20g (¾oz) of white sugarpaste into three and model oval shapes. Stick into position on the bottom half of the face just under the eye sockets and then use a cocktail stick to indent three holes on each side. For their mouths, split 5g (just under ¼oz) of white sugarpaste into three, roll into sausage shapes and round off at either end. Bend gently in the centre and stick in position underneath each muzzle.

15 Roll small oval shapes for the eyes and press down to flatten slightly. Stick in place with edible glue. Add a small,

circular black pupil to each eye, taking care to stick them in line with either the top or bottom of each eye. Roll minute sausages of black for eyelashes and attach in place.

16 Add a small, pink oval for the nose and pinch it gently at the bottom. Insert white stamens or thick thread cut to size into each hole on either side of each muzzle. (Remember to remove these before the cake is eaten.)

Assembly

17 Place one of the white kitten's bodies to the front of the cake card at an angle. Split 45g (1½oz) of white sugarpaste in half to make the two front legs. Roll into sausage shapes and then roll near the end of each to round off the paw. Push the back of a knife into the paw twice and then texture as before. Stick these two front legs in position. Push the dowel into the kitten's head that has the hole in the back and then insert the opposite end into the kitten's body.

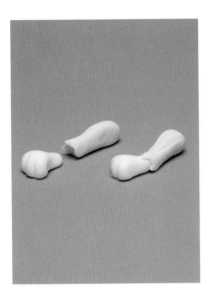

18 To make the back legs, split 45g (1½oz) of white sugarpaste in half and roll into thick sausage shapes. Bend each end round and pinch out a heel at the back. Roll gently at the ankle to narrow and round off the heel. Indent the paws as before and then stick in position. Texture the fur effect.

19 Once the first kitten is assembled, make the ears. Split 10g (¼oz) of sugarpaste in half and model two teardrop shapes. Press down onto the centre of each to make an indent and push up a small ridge around the point for the top of each ear. Fill with a small, flattened teardrop of pink paste and then cut straight at the bottom. Stick each ear in place, turned slightly towards the back, and texture as before.

20 Assemble the blue kitten against the white kitten, using a dowel to hold the head onto the body. Make blue legs with white paws and texture as before. Make the ears, bending one round slightly ready for the striped kitten's paw.

21 For the striped kitten, make the ears and legs and assemble as before, sticking the front paw playfully onto the blue kitten's ear. Add small strips of pale blue sugarpaste trimmings in varying lengths for the striped fur effect and texture as before.

22 Add tiny teardrop-shaped pieces for the tufts of fur between their ears. For the tails, use the remaining white and blue sugarpaste (around 15g/½oz for each) and roll into long sausage shapes which taper slightly at one end. Stick in position and hold for a few moments until secure.

tip

If you prefer not to use cut flower stamens for whiskers, just indented holes would suffice or make ultra thin pastillage sugar sticks (see page 15), leave to dry and insert carefully into the indented holes.

Variations

These kittens look just as cute in pink or black and white, or in grey, ginger or tortoiseshell – you could even make a whole litter in different colours!

paw print cupcakes

Extra/alternative requirements for each cupcake:

Edibles

Cupcake

A little cake filling (see recipes on pages 12 to 13)

Sugarpaste:

tiny amount black

20g (¾) sugarpaste for covering the top (these are shades of blue)

Equipment

Circle cutter (to fit cupcake once shaped with cake filling)

Nos. 4 and 18 piping nozzles (tips) (PME)

1 Take a standard size cupcake and spread cake filling over the top in a dome shape. Cover with a thin layer of sugarpaste cut to size.

2 To make the prints, cut black circles from very thinly rolled out sugarpaste using the tips of no. 18 and no. 4 plain piping nozzles. Press the circles into the top of the cupcake, grouping them together into a paw print pattern and securing with a tiny amount of edible glue.

baby's first doll

I kept this doll simply decorated to appeal to very young children, plus it's relatively easy to make. It was inspired by the toddler stage, when they lift up their little chins and stretch out their arms, waiting expectantly to be swept up for a cuddle.

Edibles

20cm (8") round cake (see recipes on pages 6 to 9)

15cm (6") dome-shaped cake (see recipes on pages 6 to 9)

400g (14oz) cake filling/crumb coat (see recipes on pages 12 to 13)

225g (8oz) marshmallow rice cereal (see recipe on page 10)

Paste food colour: white (SK)

Dust food colour: pale pink (SK)

Sugarpaste (rolled fondant):

315g (11oz) blue

pea-sized piece black

15g (½oz) dark pink

160g (5½oz) pale yellow

685g (1lb 8oz) pink

595g (1lb 5oz) soft beige

Edible glue (see recipe on page 15) (SK)

Equipment

Basic equipment (see pages 16 to 18)

30cm (12") round cake board

3 x food-safe plastic dowels

Fine and medium paintbrushes (SK)

5cm (2") circle cutter

Large heart-shaped cutter

A few cocktail sticks

Piping nozzle (tip): no. 18 (PME)

Cake Board

1 Knead the blue sugarpaste until it is soft and pliable. Sprinkle the work surface with icing sugar, rub a little onto the top of the sugarpaste and then roll out, moving the paste around to prevent sticking after each roll, until you have a thickness of 2-3mm (⅛") and the paste is large enough to cover the cake board.

2 Moisten the cake board with a little cooled, boiled water or edible glue and then lift and position the sugarpaste onto the board. Smooth the surface with a cake smoother, trim the excess from around the edge and then set aside to dry.

Doll's Head

3 Make the marshmallow rice cereal following the recipe. Whilst the mixture is still warm, mould it into an oval shape measuring 10cm x 13cm (4" x 5"). Place this down on the work surface and roll it back and forth gently so one side flattens slightly; this area will be the doll's face.

4 To make a hole for the dowel that will support the head on the body, push a dowel into the bottom whilst the mixture is still a little soft. Push the dowel in 5cm (2"), remove and put the head aside for around ten minutes to set.

5 Once the head has set firm, use small pieces of soft beige sugarpaste to fill in any uneven areas, using a little edible glue to stick them in place. Alternatively, spread a thin layer of ganache over the surface. This will create a smooth surface ready for the sugarpaste covering.

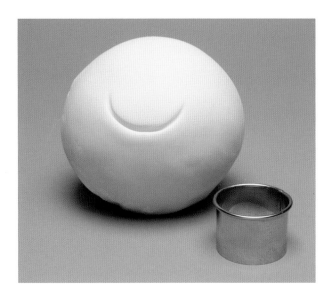

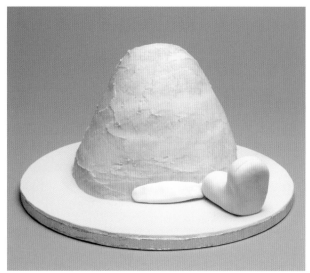

6 Brush the surface of the head with a little edible glue (unless you have used ganache). Roll out 175g (6oz) of soft beige sugarpaste and use this to cover the face and lower half of the head. To remove the ridge around the edge, smooth it with your fingertips until level with the surface. Pinch gently at the bottom of the face to shape a small chin and indent the smile using the circle cutter, pushing in at an upward angle. Use the end of a paintbrush to dimple the corners of the mouth.

7 Add a small, oval-shaped nose using the sugarpaste trimmings. Roll two tiny black oval shapes for the eyes and press each one flat. For the highlight on each eye, add a tiny dot of white food colour at the one o'clock position using a fine paintbrush. To complete the face, use your fingertip to rub a little pink dust colour over her cheeks.

Body

8 Trim the crust from each cake and level the tops. Cut a layer in each cake and then place the dome-shaped cake centrally on top of the round cake. To shape the sides, slice down and around the cake trimming away the join and slicing down to the bottom edge. Trim more at the front to make it slightly flatter.

9 Fill each layer with cake filling and then spread a thin layer over the surface of the cake to help the sugarpaste stick. Position the cake on the cake board slightly towards the back but not too far, leaving room for the dress. Roll the white sugarpaste into a tapering sausage shape no longer than 5cm (2") and use this for her knickers at the front.

Legs

10 Split 260g (9oz) of soft beige modelling paste in half. To make a leg, roll one piece into a sausage and bend round one end to make the foot. Pinch gently to narrow the foot and then mark a line around the foot using a knife. Mark small lines for the fabric effect pleats using the tip of the knife. Stick the legs in position on the cake board either side of her knickers.

Dress

11 Roll out 600g (1lb 5¼oz) of pink sugarpaste to a diameter of 30cm (12") and smooth around the cut edge with your fingertip. Place the rolling pin in the centre of the rolled-out paste, fold the back half of the paste over the pin and lift carefully. Place the paste against the cake and unroll the paste over the top, letting the back half drop down. Smooth around the dress, encouraging pleats to form, then smooth the paste further using your fingertips.

tip

If the dress stretches or distorts, cut away the excess paste using small scissors.

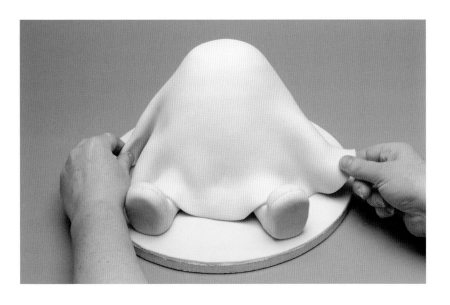

Arms

12 To help support the arms, insert two dowels on either side of the dress at an angle. To make the arms, roll the remaining soft beige modelling paste into a fat sausage measuring 14cm (5½") in length. Make sure the ends are rounded then cut it in half. Moisten each dowel and the area where the arms will sit with edible glue and then push each arm in position and hold for a few moments until secure. Mark a line around each arm in the same way as for the legs.

13 Split 60g (2oz) of pink sugarpaste in half and roll the two pieces into flattened sausage shapes measuring 13cm (5") each. Stick these in position around the top of each arm to make the sleeves. For the collar, roll out the remaining pink sugarpaste and shape a circle 8cm (3") in diameter. Cut a small 'v' in the front and round off the cut edge with your fingertips. Add this to the top of the cake and secure with a little edible glue.

14 Roll out the dark pink sugarpaste and cut the large heart shape for the front of the dress. Stick this in place with edible glue. Using the same paste, cut out circles with a no. 18 piping nozzle to decorate the cake board. Press each one gently into the surface to soften the edges.

15 Push the dowel down through the cake, leaving 5cm (2") protruding at the top. Position the head down onto it, securing at the base with edible glue.

Hair

16 Thinly roll out the pale yellow sugarpaste and cut strips in varying lengths measuring around 1cm (³/₈") wide. Add them to the head little by little, starting from the centre and making a centre parting all the way down the back of the head. When the head is completely covered, cut smaller strips for the fringe and her two bunches and secure in place.

baby's first doll   99

baby's first doll

mini doll cakes

Extra/alternative requirements for each doll:

Edibles

Cupcake

A little cake filling (see recipes on pages 12 to 13)

Sugarpaste (rolled fondant):

75g (2½oz) soft beige or golden brown (for the head, arms and legs)

45g (1½oz) blue, dark pink or light pink (for the dress)

30g (1oz) blue, dark pink or light pink (for the cake card)

5g (just under ¼oz) blue, dark pink or light pink (for the heart)

Equipment

10cm (4") round cake card

Lolly stick

2cm (¾") circle cutter

Small heart-shaped cutter

tip

If you would prefer to use less sugarpaste to decorate these mini dolls, I recommend you use truffle mixture or marshmallow rice cereal mixture inside each head and then cover with sugarpaste instead of using a solid ball of sugarpaste (see below).

1 Cover a 10cm (4") round cake card with sugarpaste in blue, light pink or dark pink.

2 Roll an oval shape for the head from 60g (2oz) of sugarpaste. Alternatively, make the shape from 30g (1oz) of cake truffle mixture or 20g (¾oz) of marshmallow rice cereal and cover with soft beige or golden brown sugarpaste (as for the large doll). Push a lolly stick into the base to make a hole and remove. Add the facial features as for the large doll.

3 Turn the cupcake upside down and trim to remove the edge then spread with a thin layer of cake filling. As this cupcake is completely flat, press a 5g (just under ¼oz) ball of sugarpaste (any colour) onto the top of the cake to round it off and to give height.

4 Make the legs from 10g (¼oz) of paste in the same way as for the large doll and stick them to the front of the cake with edible glue.

5 Measure the cupcake and roll out a circle of sugarpaste to cover it. Make the dress and decorate as before.

6 Make the arms from sugarpaste as for the large doll. Split 5g (just under ¼oz) of the dress paste in half for the sleeves and use another 5g (just under ¼oz) for the collar, following the same method as for the large doll. This time use a 2cm (¾") circle cutter for the collar.

7 Finish each doll by making strands for the hair and sticking them in place, as for the large doll. Push the lolly stick down through the body and secure the head in place with edible glue.

tip

If you are short of time or have lots of mini dolls to make, you can simplify the feet by rolling 5g (just under ¼oz) oval shapes of coloured sugarpaste to look like shoes. You can also cut down the time needed to make the hair by rolling a tiny spiral of coloured sugarpaste to create a simple but effective single baby curl.

noah's ark

Here's a pretty, pastel-coloured depiction of the biblical Noah's Ark, with cute baby-style animals two-by-two, perfect for any small child's celebration.

Edibles

20cm (8") round cake (see recipes on pages 6 to 9)

20cm (8") bowl-shaped cake (see recipes on pages 6 to 9)

2 x 10cm (4") square cakes (see recipes on pages 6 to 9)

685g (1lb 8oz) cake filling/crumb coat (see recipes on pages 12 to 13)

Sugarpaste (rolled fondant):

260g (9oz) pale blue

1.14kg (2lb 8oz) pale lemon

60g (2oz) white

Modelling paste:

2g (½oz) black

20g (¾oz) pale blue

75g (2½oz) pale brown

145g (5oz) pale golden brown

340g (12oz) pale grey

110g (3¾oz) pale pink

5g (just under ¼oz) white

145g (5oz) yellow

Edible glue (see recipe on page 15) (SK)

Equipment

Basic equipment (see pages 16 to 18)

20cm (8") round cake board

12cm and 18cm (5" and 7") round thin cake cards/boards

6 x food-safe plastic dowels

3cm (1¼") round circle cutter

4 x paper lolly sticks

A few cocktail sticks

Cakes

1 Trim the crust from all four cakes and level the tops. Place the round cake on top of the bowl-shaped cake and trim the sides so the join is neat. Trim around the top edge to taper in to exactly 18cm (7") in diameter. Lift the round cake off, cut layers in each cake and sandwich with cake filling. Place the round cake on top of the smaller cake card.

2 Place the bowl-shaped cake onto the centre of the cake board. Push three dowels down into the cake keeping them quite central and no more than 8cm (3") apart. Mark each one level with the top of the cake and then remove. Cut the dowels to the lowest mark (this ensures that even if the cake isn't level, subsequent layers will be). Push the cut dowels back into the cake. Place the round cake back onto the bowl-shaped cake and then spread a layer of cake filling over the whole cake to seal it and help the sugarpaste stick.

3 Roll out 125g (4½oz) of lemon sugarpaste, cover the larger cake card completely and trim away the excess from around the edge. Dowel the round cake as before, keeping the dowels central and around 10cm (4") apart. Place the covered cake card onto the top (if there is a small gap between the card and the cake, fill with a little cake filling so the surface is smooth prior to covering).

4 To make the cabin, place the two 10cm square cakes one on top of the other. Trim one side by 1cm (³⁄₈"), making the cake slightly oblong. Cut the roof shape from the longest side, cutting down to

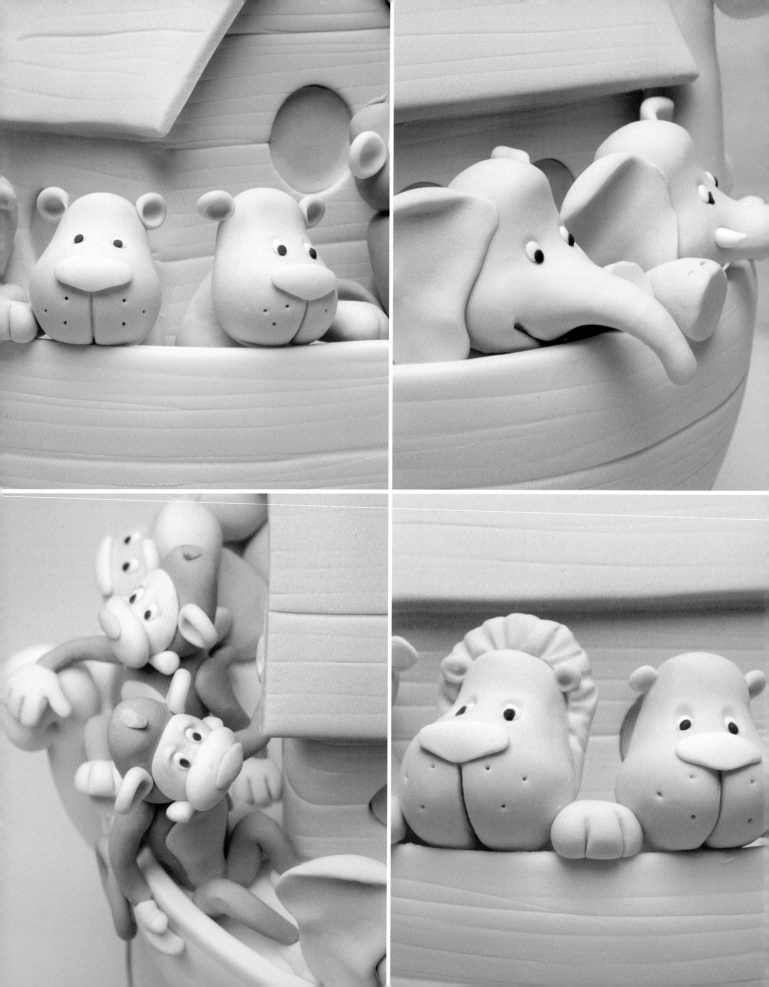

mini ark cakes

These mini cakes are made using standard size cupcakes.

Extra/alternative requirements for each ark:

Edibles

Cupcake

A little cake filling (see recipes on pages 12 to 13)

Sugarpaste (rolled fondant):

   100g (3½oz) pale blue

   10g (¼oz) pale pink

Modelling paste:

   tiny piece black

   tiny piece green

   5g (just under ¼oz) white

   tiny piece yellow

1 Level the top of the cupcake, cut a layer in the centre and fill with cake filling. This will increase the height a little. Either brush some warm jam over the surface to help the sugarpaste stick or use a little cake filling.

2 Cover the top of the cake first and then the sides, keeping the paste a little higher than the top to create a lip. The main cake was covered in two halves which you can do for the mini cakes too, but if you have a large number to make then you may find rolling the paste around the whole cake is quicker. Shape the top of the ark as before but measuring 2.5cm (1") square with a height of 4cm (1½").

3 If you would like your recipients to keep the little birdhouse then I recommend sticking the bird onto the top so they can keep this also. Make the bird as per the previous instructions; if you would like to make a dove, make it from white modelling paste and add the green branch depicting the new growth where land had been found.

mini animal cakes

These mini animal cakes are really easy to make, ideal for getting the children involved at a party. If you don't have the silicone bakeware you could also use stainless steel sundae dishes or small, ovenproof glass bowls available from kitchenware specialists or the homeware department in most supermarkets.

Extra/alternative requirements for each animal:

Edibles

Mini cake in 7cm (2¾") ovenproof dome-shaped silicone bowl or moulds

A little cake filling or jam (see recipe on pages 12 to 13)

Sugarpaste (rolled fondant):

    35g (1¼oz) in your choice of colour (depending on the animal you are making)

Modelling paste:

    Around 30g (1oz) for each animal head (monkey has 5g (just under ¼oz) more for the tail)

Equipment

7cm (2¾") cake card or circle of greaseproof paper

1 Place the cake on a thin cake card or use a disc of greaseproof paper the same size as the cake to protect the uncovered cake underneath. Use a little cake filling or warm jam (this spreads a little easier) over the surface and then roll out the sugarpaste to cover the cake. Smooth the paste around the shape.

2 Use a knife to trim the excess paste away or tuck it underneath for a more rounded look. If you have lots of cakes to do, you could use a circle cutter the same size as the covered cake and press down to cut the excess away quickly and easily.

3 Make a head following instructions from the main cake and stick it to the cake with edible glue.

templates

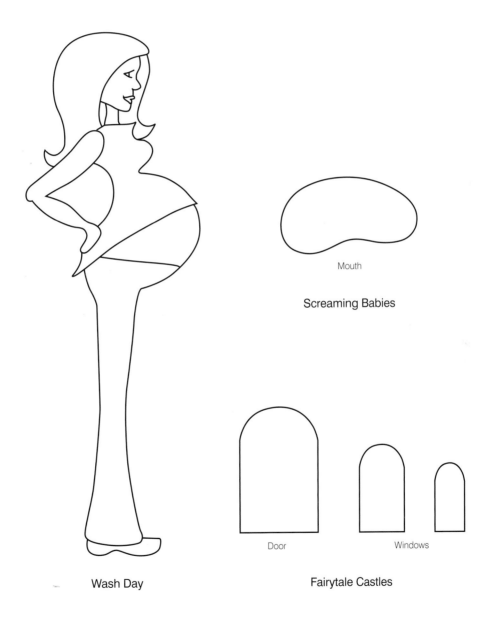

Mouth

Screaming Babies

Wash Day

Door   Windows

Fairytale Castles

Suppliers

Squires Kitchen

Squires Kitchen, UK
3 Waverley Lane
Farnham
Surrey
GU9 8BB
0845 61 71 810
+44 (0) 1252 260 260
www.squires-shop.com

Squires Kitchen International School
The Grange
Hones Yard
Farnham
Surrey
GU9 8BB
0845 61 71 810
+44 (0) 1252 260 260
www.squires-school.co.uk

Squires Kitchen, France
+33 (0) 1 82 88 01 66
clientele@squires-shop.fr
www.squires-shop.fr

Squires Kitchen, Spain
+34 93 180 7382
cliente@squires-shop.es
www.squires-shop.es

Debbie Brown Ltd.

debra.brown@btinternet.com
www.debbiebrownscakes.co.uk

Shops

UK
Decor 4 Cakes Ltd.
Essex
01255 422031

Jane Asher Party Cakes
London
www.jane-asher.co.uk

Pipedreams
Berkshire
www.pipedreams-sugarcraft.co.uk

Sugar Celebrations
Wiltshire and Gloucester
www.sugarcelebrations.com

Australia
Cakedeco
Victoria
+61 (0) 3 9654 5335
cakedeco@optusnet.com.au

Iced Affair
New South Wales
www.icedaffair.com.au

Susie Q Cake Decorating Centre
Victoria
www.susie-qcake.com.au

Canada
SugarTiers Inc.
Ontario
www.sugartiers.ca

Greece
Sugar World - Aliprantis Ltd.
Athens
www.sugarworld.gr

Italy
Marzipan World
Sesto Calende (Va)
www.marzipanworld.com

Malaysia
International Centre of Cake Artistry Sdn. Bhd.
Selangor
www.2decoratecakes.com

The Netherlands
Planet Cake®
Rotterdam
www.cake.nl

Nigeria
Kogsy Merchandise
Lagos
www.kogsycakeandsugarcraft.com

Poland
Tortownia
Warszawa
www.tortownia.pl

Sweden
Kungälv
www.tartdecor.se

Manufacturers and Distributors

UK
Ceefor Cakes
PO Box 443
Leighton Buzzard
Bedfordshire
LU7 1AJ
01525 375237
info@ceeforcakes.co.uk
www.ceeforcakes.co.uk

Confectionery Supplies
Herefordshire
www.confectionerysupplies.co.uk

Food Packaging & Cakeboards Ltd.
Lancashire
www.fpcb.co.uk

Guy, Paul & Co. Ltd.
Buckinghamshire
www.guypaul.co.uk

Australia
Zoratto Enterprises
New South Wales
www.wilton-australia.com

New Zealand
See Zoratto Enterprises, Australia

USA
Beryl's Cake Decorating & Pastry Supplies
Springfield, VA
www.beryls.com

Caljava International School of Cake Decorating and Sugar Craft
Northridge, CA
www.cakevisions.com

Global Sugar Art, LLC
Plattsburgh, NY
+1-800-420-6088
www.globalsugarart.com

Guilds

The British Sugarcraft Guild
Wellington House
Messeter Place
London
SE9 5DP
020 8859 6943
www.bsguk.org